Saints and Sinners

An Insider's Guide to Bible People
and Their Times

Gerald Wheeler

REVIEW AND HERALD® PUBLISHING ASSOCIATION
HAGERSTOWN, MD 21740

The author assumes full responsibility for the accuracy
of all facts and quotations as cited in this book.

Unless noted otherwise, Scripture references are from the New Revised
Standard Version of the Bible, copyright © 1989 by the Division of Christian
Education of the National Council of the Churches of Christ in the U.S.A.
Used by permission.
Texts credited to KJV are from the King James Version of the Bible.

This book was
Edited by Raymond H. Woolsey
Copyedited by Jocelyn Fay and James Cavil
Designed by Bill Kirstein
Electronic makeup by Shirley M. Bolivar
Cover design by Bill Kirstein
Typeset: 11/13 Minion

PRINTED IN U.S.A.

04 03 02 01 00   5 4 3 2 1

R&H Cataloging Service
Wheeler, Gerald William, 1943-
    Saints and sinners: an insider's guide to Bible people and their times.

    1. Bible—Biography.   I. Title.

            220.92

ISBN 0-8280-1572-4

Dedication

∾

To James Estes,
whose life has been a
biography of praise to all who
know him.

Also by Gerald Wheeler:
  Beyond Life
  Wisdom

  To order, call **1-800-765-6955.**
  Visit our Web site at *www.reviewandherald.com* for information on other Review and Herald products.

Contents

CHAPTER 1

The Celestial Opponents

Many people think of the Bible as a collection of religious rules, commands, principles, and devotional thoughts. Others regard it as only a book of theology or a series of sermons. And Scripture does contain these things. But most of all, it is the stories of people. The Bible is full of accounts of men, women, and children just like you and me. They love or hate, feel joy or grief, triumph against adversity or make mistakes and fail, rebel or repent—all the things people still do today. Religion is not an intellectual abstraction—it is lived out in daily experience, whether in lofty deeds or the commonplace incidents of ordinary life. Unlike most of us, though, the people of the Bible lived with a constant awareness of God's presence in their lives.

But more than just reports of human beings, the Bible is also a narrative of the God who created them and longs to save them from the rebellion that the human family freely chose for itself. Scripture is the story of a God of love wooing the objects of His love and helping them to resist the one who led them away from Him.

The Bible is about persons, whether they be supernatural or human. Religion is the story of people and their God, not philosophical abstractions. Thus Scripture is, in reality, biography.

When the biblical authors wrote about people, though, they approached their subjects from a slightly different perspective than we do today. They were not interested in in-depth psychological studies of individual personalities. Except for the Old Testament patriarchs (particularly Jacob) and David, Scripture does not present full, detailed biographies. Even the Gospel accounts of Jesus do not include many of the things we would want to know about a person today.

The concerns of the biblical writers differed from those of modern biographers. To a large extent, the authors of the Scriptures see the people they write about as illustrations of some fundamental principle of life and reality. The incidents they record depict the outworking of loyalty or betrayal, of courage or cowardice, of generosity or greed. The Bible shows what it means to be good or evil in daily life. By modern standards biblical biographies are terse and bare-boned. Biblical writers focused on specific aspects of a person's life and ignored what they considered irrelevant (no matter how interesting it might be to us) to the point that they wanted to make. Each word, phrase, or scene concentrates on the divine truth Scripture seeks to reveal. Through its often cryptic approach the Bible forces us to think, to search deeply and carefully for the message it sees revealed in each life it considers.

In this book we will examine selected examples of some of the Bible's biographies. Often we will group them by theme or subject. Because these individuals lived in a world and culture in many ways vastly different from today, we have provided some of the biblical background to help understand what they did and what motivated them. We will briefly look at the customs and sociology that shaped the various people of the Bible.

Selfless Love Versus Selfishness

While we will deal with all kinds of people, in a fundamental way Scripture is in reality the overarching story of two individuals, neither of them human. Sometimes they interact directly with humanity, most times behind the scenes. The two beings represent two totally opposite perspectives. One focuses on the needs of others; the other exists only for himself. Both, strangely enough, are beings of love. Christ's love is always directed outward, while Satan's has turned permanently inward. The first demonstrates what love must be to have a happy universe. The other reveals what happens to love when it becomes debased and warped.

The Bible presents God first. We don't need anyone to teach us about evil—it is part of our very nature. But sin has blinded us to God and goodness. As a consequence we must know God before we can resist evil—or even recognize its more insidious forms.

Ancient religions often focused on evil. They sought to know how to manipulate the demons and other beings they believed were responsible for inflicting disease, pain, and suffering upon humanity. Thus in many religions the study of magic replaced true worship. Such religious observances did not transform lives for the better or seek to bring the worshiper into an intimate relationship with deity. The great national religions of Egypt and other ancient Middle Eastern civilizations were not personal ones. They were political institutions. The priests helped the gods fight back the forces of chaos that threatened to destroy the world around them. Sometimes the priests attempted to control the gods themselves for human advantage.

The gods cared nothing about people as individuals and had little concern about how human beings behaved. Religion had little sense of morality, ethics, or devotion. The gods could be as immoral as human beings. They just had more power than we did. If even the gods were evil, how could human beings sense their own fallen natures? They had nothing of real goodness to compare themselves against. We cannot grasp the full danger and implications of evil until we can compare it to good. And to know good we must know God, for only He is good (Mark 10:18).

Evil is only and always a distortion of good. But once we have become evil we can no longer see good. It warps our spiritual eyesight so that we can never again see clearly. God must reveal goodness to us and then enable us to recognize it. Thus God had to enter our sinful world and show us what He and goodness are like.

Some religions, such as Zoroastrianism, have taught that good and evil have always existed side by side, in some cases forever struggling for dominance. But Scripture reveals that evil did not always exist. It is only a temporary aberration in a universe created good by a good and perfect God (Gen. 1:31). Someday it will be eradicated (Rev. 21:1-5; Nahum 1:9; Isa. 65:17; 2 Peter 3:13). Evil created itself when a perfect being chose no longer to be perfect. Why Satan made that decision will forever remain inexplicable. Sin is a mystery beyond human understanding.

The Bible is thus from beginning to end the story of good and evil and the beings who lead each side of the cosmic struggle between the two powers. It is the biography of a good God and a fallen, rebellious creation of that perfect deity, and the impact they both have on the universe. In some ways the Bible presents shadow biographies of God and Satan. We see more their influence than either of them directly. But they are still there throughout Scripture. More important, the Bible unveils the role played by one particular member of the Godhead, Jesus the Christ, as He seeks to resolve the crisis caused by Satan's rebellion and the new element that the devil introduced into the universe: sin.

No Reason for Sin

Sin—deliberate disobedience and perversion of all that is good—is such a part of human reality that we cannot imagine existence any other way. That is why some have concluded that not only has it always existed but it must serve some purpose in the universe. Without sin, some argue, we would not know what good is. Others suggest that God uses evil to mature and develop human beings.[1] One Christian cult taught that God let humanity stumble into sin so that He could demonstrate human limitations. Paul Helm reasons that the fall of the human race "is happy because it, and it alone, makes possible the divine redemption from which the blessings of pardon and renewal follow. . . . The states of forgiveness and of renewal and all that these imply are of greater overall good than a state of primitive innocence. . . . Finally, without the permission of moral evil, and the atonement of Christ, God's own character would not be fully manifest."[2] The great Reformer John Calvin boldly claimed that humanity's fall gave God greater glory.[3]

But in the words of John Sanders, "there is no good reason for sin; in fact, it is highly implausible given all that God has done" for His creation.[4] Elsewhere he comments that according to a relational model of salvation, "sin is a broken relationship with God. When we fail to trust in God's good provision for us and reject the boundaries in which he placed us, we are refusing to respond in love to the divine love. This is irrational because there is no good reason not to trust God. . . . In this sense sin has no cause. If it did, then it would not be blameworthy and it could be readily prevented or corrected." [5]

Truth and Falsehood

Yet we all know that sin does exist. It should not, but it infects every aspect of life. Sin distorts our understanding of reality and blocks our ability to grasp truth. The Bible not only is the biographies of good and evil—it also reveals truth and falsehood. In the unfallen universe truth is the way things are; on our sin-corrupted earth it is the way things would be if sin did not exist. God created the universe to function in certain ways that we can sum up as love. Because creation should reflect the God who made it, truth is ultimately God Himself. The New Testament often equates truth with Jesus Christ (John 14:6) or the Holy Spirit (1 John 5:6). When Christians search for truth, they are not really seeking facts and intellectual propositions, but the Person behind them. Jesus came to depict more fully God and the reality He and the Father created before the entrance of sin. Christ told Philip, "Whoever has seen me has seen the Father" (John 14:9). The Godhead and its members—the Father, Son, and Holy Spirit—are truth.

A lie, on the other hand, is a deliberate altering or misrepresentation of truth—and ultimately of God Himself. It tries to warp reality, to twist it into what the deceiver would like it to be. At the tree of the knowledge of good and evil Satan distorted both God and human beings. He raised questions about God's nature and worked to convince Adam and Eve that they were more than they really were—that they could become like God Himself (Gen. 3:1-7). He still argues that God is a tyrant and that human beings are immortal, with godlike powers hidden within them. Satan's lies deceived many in heaven (John 8:44; Rev. 12:7-9) and have most of the human race in their thrall. The devil is both the original liar and the greatest lie. He is no longer what

11

God created, but what he made of himself.

The conflict between God and Satan, between good and evil, is also between truth and lies. Lies are so tempting because they appear to make the world the way we would like it to be. Satan deceived himself, and now he deceives others. He is falsehood, and Christ is truth.

The Accuser

The Old Testament was cautious about mentioning Satan. It makes only a few references to him. The Hebrew noun *satan* describes acts of obstruction, opposition, or accusation.[6] As a figure or person the *satan* appears only a few times. In Job 1 and 2 he calls the patriarch Job a fraud and demands that the man be put to the test to prove what he is really like. Satan accuses the high priest Joshua of being a sinner in Zechariah 3:2. Also (without the definite article before the noun) he incites David to conduct a census in 1 Chronicles 21:1, apparently encouraging the king to trust in his military resources rather than the power of God. Bible commentators have interpreted several other figures in the Old Testament as depicting Satan. Many consider the serpent of Genesis 3 as a manifestation or agent of the devil. The lying or deceiving spirit of 1 Kings 22:19-23 has often been seen as a satanic figure. In addition, Christian biblical interpretation has historically regarded Isaiah 14:12-15 and Ezekiel 28 as allusions to Satan's fall from heaven.[7]

Although the Old Testament portrays Satan as an accuser of God's people, it does not emphasize his power or even stress his opposition to God that much. Perhaps one of the reasons it does not make a big point about Satan is that the people of the ancient world were too familiar with stories of contending pagan gods. Egyptian religion told of two divine brothers, Horus and Seth, who fought each other for rulership of the gods. The pair were roughly of equal power, and Egyptians long worshiped both of them.

Horus, through much struggle, convinced the other gods to make him king after his brother Seth had killed their father.[8] Despite Seth's evil nature, since the dawn of Egyptian history

Egyptians had worshiped him at Naqada, one of the largest pre-dynastic sites, and in the northeastern Nile delta, which would have been not too far north of the land of Goshen, where the Hebrews had lived. The Asiatic conquerors of Egypt, the Hyksos, worshiped him, and Egyptians considered Seth to be the god of foreign lands, including Palestine. The Ramesside kings especially venerated him.[9] Rulers such as Seti I and Sethnakhte took their names from the god.[10] Canaanite gods also struggled with each other, often in quite bloodthirsty ways, and the Hebrews would be exposed to them when they entered the Promised Land, reinforcing the concept of gods vying for supremacy.

Had the Lord in the Old Testament talked more openly about the opposition between Him and Satan, God's people might have interpreted it in light of the many pagan stories about supernatural beings battling for supremacy. They could have considered Satan an equal with God, comparable to Seth or the demons and deities of other religions. Pagans often worshiped evil gods and demons so as to control them. The fact that evil is so persuasive could have tempted the Israelites to worship Satan in an attempt to protect themselves from his power.

The New Testament has much more to say about Satan. He both originated and now instigates sin. First John 3:8 declares that "everyone who commits sin is a child of the devil; for the devil has been sinning from the beginning." Echoing Isaiah 14 and Ezekiel 28, Revelation 12:7, 8 confirms that Satan once belonged to the divine realm, but rebelled against God. The Godhead had to exile him and his followers. After Satan came to the earth and seduced the first couple, he assumed the roles of tempter (Matt. 4:3), enemy (Matt. 13:37-39), adversary (1 Peter 5:8), and deceiver (Rev. 12:9) of humanity.

Satan's constant goal has been to lead the human race into total rebellion against God. Yet even as he does so he defames God's people before God Himself (Rev. 12:10).

The apostle Paul warned believers not to let Satan outwit them (2 Cor. 2:11), especially by losing self-control (1 Cor. 7:5). Paul explained that Satan could work either through human agents, "the lawless one" (2 Thess. 2:3, 4, 9), or he could appear as a supernatural being, disguising himself as "an angel of light" (2 Cor. 11:14). But Christ's power was greater than that of Satan or his agents. He could compel Satan's evil agents to release their victims (Matt. 8:16; Mark 1:39). And the book of Revelation reveals that Christ will triumph over Satan in the end (Rev. 20:1-3, 7-10).

The God Who Veils Himself

Strangely, just as the Old Testament says little about Satan it is also reticent about Jesus. Perhaps it downplays Jesus as a separate member of the Godhead for a reason similar to why it was cautious in speaking of Satan. In a polytheistic world in which people chose the god or gods they worshiped, the Lord did not want to confuse His people. They would have a hard time distinguishing between the Trinity and the pagan concepts of families of deities.[11] Even the Christian church has struggled for centuries to come to an understanding of the Trinity and the relationship of its members. The God of Israel first wanted His people to grasp who alone was all-powerful and earn their trust and loyalty. The nature of the Godhead was something that He could reveal more fully later.

In time the second member of the Godhead emptied Himself of His outward manifestation of deity (Phil. 2:5-8) and incarnated Himself in human form (John 1:14). Jesus was born (Luke 2:6) and grew as any other human child (verse 52). He worked at the carpenter's trade, then spent three years teaching and healing. Eventually the religious and political authorities killed Him. The Gospels record a theological interpretation of His life, and the rest of the New Testament is a commentary on that life's meaning for us. Those around Him had seen little more than a human being, though they sensed that He was not just another human being (see, for example, Mark 4:41). But after His resurrection and ascension His followers struggled to grasp the fact that He was far more than they had ever assumed.

Jesus has always been the God who veils Himself. It was most likely He who came to Abraham in human form as the patriarch sat outside his tent (Gen. 18). God in the guise of a human being told Abraham and Sarah that they would have a child, and He bargained with Abraham over the fate of Sodom.[12] The angel of the Lord frequently appeared to human beings. He came to Moses in the burning bush (Ex. 3; the angel of the Lord is in the bush [verse 2] and the Lord calls to Moses "out of" the burning bush [verse 4]). Also the angel of the Lord revealed Himself to Gideon (Judges 6:11-18) and the parents of Samson (Judges 13).

Humanity cannot see God and live (Ex. 33:20), so God always has to assume some form that will not endanger His creation. But Christ especially veils Himself in humble guises.[13] He let His human life point to the Father rather than Himself (John 5:19; 12:49; 14:10). Satan tried to be more than he was (Isa. 14:13, 14), but Christ is willing to be seen as less than He really is. The One who created the world (John 1:3; Col. 1:15, 16) was willing to walk that world as part of His own creation. The Creator became a creature to redeem them. And for eternity He will be one with His redeemed as the nail-scarred Jesus.

Trying to Describe an Infinite God

The most real things in the world are often the most difficult to depict. For example, how do you describe love? We can only compare it to things we already know. Thus we might compare love to a warm hug, a gentle touch, a mother who gets up in the middle of the night to nurse a sick child. None of these illustrations can capture all that love is, but at least they present some aspect of it that we can grasp because we have experienced whatever particular thing love has been compared to. The list of images of what love is like can be endless because love itself is infinite and complex. Thus we use analogies, metaphors, and all kinds of figures of speech to communicate the illusive but very real nature of something that we can describe no other way.

God is even more infinite and complex. The Bible employs a broad range of comparisons and analogies to give us glimpses of what God is like. No comparison can catch all that God or Jesus or the Holy Spirit is. Jesus is the Good Shepherd (John 10:14)—

and more. He calls Himself the gate to the sheepfold (John 10:7), the Bread of Life (John 6:35), the Bridegroom (Matt. 9:15), the Lamb of God (John 1:29), and the True Vine (John 15:1). Scripture portrays Him as friend, teacher, healer, guest, host, Suffering Servant, Anointed One, and Saviour. Each image captures only a fragment of all that He is. Even all of them together but hint at His infiniteness. But without such images we could know nothing about Jesus.

Who Is Qualified to Be God?

One of the major issues of the biblical depiction of the conflict between good and evil is the question of who alone is qualified to be God. Isaiah 14 depicts the Day Star (Lucifer) as declaring, "I will ascend to heaven; I will raise my throne above the stars of God; I will sit on the mount of assembly on the heights of Zaphon; I will ascend to the tops of the clouds, I will make myself like the Most High" (Isa. 14:13, 14). The passage uses the ancient imagery of the divine assembly, and Lucifer wants to be over it all. When he couldn't achieve that, he tempted Adam and Eve with his own longing (Gen. 3). Sinful beings want to be their own gods.

What all creation must satisfy in its mind is not only who should be in charge of the universe but even more important, who alone is capable of ruling and sustaining it. Only God can bring new kinds of life into existence. And only He has the power, the love, and the goodness to rule and elicit loyalty from beings with free will. God alone is self-existent. Satan and humans are created beings, their existence sustained and totally dependent on the Creator of the universe. They are also sinful and self-centered. Self-centered creatures by their very nature cannot really care for others. Such beings think only of themselves. Every day as we watch the news—and even experience in our own lives—we see what evil can motivate fallen creatures to do to others. Satan destroys others to get his way. But Christ died to save His creation. Satan thinks only of himself, while Christ's every thought is of love toward His creation.

God deserves worship because He is love in action. Satan

brought sin and death, while Christ's death led to renewed life for humanity. God is love; Satan is hate. Christ transforms His followers into godlike reflections of Himself. Satan makes demons into his image. In Revelation 19:13 Christ wears a robe dipped in blood, an allusion to His sacrifice on the cross. Inscribed on that robe is "King of kings and Lord of lords" (verse 16). Christ can wear the title because He has demonstrated who alone is both worthy and capable of governing a universe of peace, joy, and love.

The Bible is the story of a world created by a good God, usurped by a rebel, then redeemed by One who veils His deity and joins Himself to His creation forever. Christ will end Satan's reign of terror. The whole universe will once again acknowledge who is truly God. It will be eternally recognized that no one else can ever take His place. And because of that conviction, sin will never rise again.

---

[1] See John Hick, *Evil and the God of Love,* rev. ed. (New York: Harper and Row, 1978).

[2] Paul Helm, *The Providence of God* (Downers Grove, Ill.: InterVarsity Press, 1994), pp. 214, 215.

[3] John Calvin, *Calvin: Institutes of the Christian Religion* (Philadelphia: Westminster Press, 1960), vol. 1, p. 196.

[4] John Sanders, *The God Who Risks: A Theology of Providence* (Downers Grove, Ill.: InterVarsity Press, 1998), p. 224.

[5] *Ibid.,* p. 243.

[6] *Dictionary of Biblical Imagery* (Downers Grove, Ill.: InterVarsity Press, 1998), p. 759.

[7] I have discussed how these passages speak of more than just their contemporary references in *Beyond Life: What God Says About Life, Death, and Immortality* (Hagerstown, Md.: Review and Herald Pub. Assn., 1998), pp. 57-60.

[8] Ian Shaw and Paul Nicholson, *The Dictionary of Ancient Egypt* (New York: Harry N. Abrams, 1995), pp. 133, 134. See also Rosalie David, *Handbook to Life in Ancient Egypt* (New York: Oxford University Press, 1998). For a popularized account of the struggle between the two gods, see M. V. Seton-Williams, *Egyptian Legends and Stories* (New York: Barnes and Noble, 1988), pp. 24-38.

[9] *Letters From Ancient Egypt.* Trans. Edward F. Wente. Ed. Edmund S. Meltzer (Atlanta: Scholars Press, 1990), p. 253.

[10] Shaw and Nicholson, *The Dictionary of Ancient Egypt,* pp. 264, 265.

[11] Egypt had a kind of trinity consisting of Amun, Re, and Ptah. See *Hymns, Prayers, and Songs: An Anthology of Ancient Egyptian Lyric Poetry.* Trans. John

L. Foster (Atlanta: Scholars Press, 1995), p. 78.

[12] Note the enigmatic way Genesis 19:24 has the Lord raining sulphur and fire "from the Lord out of heaven," implying two Lords, one on earth and the other in heaven.

[13] The Holy Spirit retreats even further into the shadows, pointing to Jesus rather than to Himself (see John 15:26; 16:13).

CHAPTER 2

The Betrayers

$\mathbf{A}$s was customary in ancient Mediterranean society, Jesus chose most of His disciples from a small group. The majority came from His adopted village, Capernaum. The inhabitants of Capernaum comprised what sociologists refer to as His in-group. A person's in-group usually consisted of one's household, extended family, and friends and neighbors. Those who belonged to such an in-group were expected to help and to be loyal to each other. They were bound to each other by close ties.[1] Those disciples who were not from Capernaum were still Galilean except for one—Judas. He was probably the only one from Judea, the area around Jerusalem and the territory of the old kingdom of Judah.

The word usually translated "Jew" (*Ioudaios*) in the New Testament really means "of or pertaining to Judea." The word *Ioudaismos*, often translated "Judaism," actually refers to "the behavior typical of and particular to those from Judea."[2] People outside of Palestine labeled those who worshiped the God of Israel as Judeans, or "Jews." Thus Paul, although he was a citizen of Tarsus, would have been considered an *Ioudaios*, that is, a Judean or "Jew." Judaism, the religion we know today, did not develop until after New Testament times. It and Christianity emerged alongside each other out of the biblical worship of the God of Israel. That is why the New Testament can say that the "Jews" (*Ioudaios*) opposed Jesus while seemingly ignoring the fact that His disciples and the crowds of people flocking to Him also were what we would consider Jews today. Scripture means that the leaders of Judea rejected Him, partly because He was a Galilean.

The people of Judea looked down on the Galileans as provincial, backward, and not as religiously devout. The Pharisees, who lived almost exclusively around Jerusalem, suspected the people of Galilee of not being as faithful in observing religious law and practice. Galileans also spoke a different dialect, which made them stand out when they visited Judea. They mispronounced guttural sounds.[3] For example, they turned the name Elazar into "Lazarus." One of the disciples, Peter, would later have his Galilean accent get him into trouble (Matt. 26:73).

In this chapter we will look at two of Jesus' disciples, one a Galilean and the other most likely from Judea.[4] Despite their cultural differences they shared something in common: both Peter and Judas would betray Jesus.

The Galilean

Peter was in some ways the stereotypical Galilean—rough and uncultured. A fisherman, he lived in the village of Bethsaida Julias, on the northeastern shore of the Sea of Galilee. Modern readers of the Gospels like to think of him as an owner and partner in a business. But that is projecting modern society into the biblical account.

Because fish was a luxury food item in New Testament times, the fishing industry attracted the interest of the wealthy. Royal concerns organized fishers to supply specific amounts of fish for designated periods. The investors paid the fishers either in cash or processed fish. Papyrus documents reveal that while the estate managers or royal coffers took in high profits, the actual fishers received little for their work. Also they had constantly to protest irregular or low payments.

Fishers also could lease fishing rights from toll or tax collectors, who collected up to 40 percent of the catch. What remained the fishers then sold to distributors, who pocketed most of the profit and drove the prices up for the consumer. The system forced up the cost of fish to the point that by the end of the second century the Romans had to pass laws that only those who actually caught the fish or bought it directly from them could offer it on the market. Tax collectors in the fishing business often had partners. Peter, Andrew, James, and John could have worked in this kind of system (Luke 5:7, 10).[5] Thus they would have had to work hard to eke out at best a meager living. It would have intensified Peter's aggressive and domineering nature. He would have been sympathetic to revolutionary movements in society that sought to overturn the oppressive economic and political systems. The Gospels depict him as constantly pushing himself forward as spokesperson for the other disciples. He carried a sword (John 18:10) and was willing to use it. Yet he was intensely loyal to Jesus.

The Judean

Judas, on the other hand, would have seemed much more cultured and impressive. Unlike the way Jesus did the other disciples, He apparently never gave Judas a specific call. Normally disciples chose the teachers they wanted to follow,[6] but Jesus selected His own students. Some students of the Bible identify the scribe of Matthew 8:19, 20 as Judas joining Jesus' band of disciples by his own choice. If this was indeed Judas, as a scribe[7] he would be much better educated than Christ's other followers. Judas had many talents and abilities and became the group's treasurer (John 12:6; 13:29). Although Jesus knew Judas' flaws (John 6:71), He permitted the disciple to stay.

One old tradition has regarded Judas as an outsider. But an honest reading of the New Testament clearly indicates that he was "a disciple of Jesus from early on" who had "the respect and confidence of the group."[8] Although Judas may have invited himself into the inner circle of disciples, Jesus treated him as one of the twelve. When He sent the disciples out to teach and heal, Judas most likely performed miracles along with the others. Scripture makes only two charges against him: he was greedy, pilfering from the common funds (John 12:6), and he turned Jesus over to His enemies.

Since Judas was possibly a scribe as well as a Judean, it must have frustrated and disappointed him greatly when Jesus criticized the priests and other leaders of Judea. He would have shared the common understanding at the time of the coming Messiah as a deliverer who would lead His people in overthrowing the Roman yoke. Judas would have believed that Jesus as Messiah would need the support of the religious leaders. And he would have been in the forefront of those who sought to make Jesus king after He fed the 5,000 (John 6:15). John Sanders suggests that Jesus may have attempted to alter Judas's understanding of His role but was no more successful with him than He was with any of the other disciples.[9] As Jesus failed to make an alliance with the Judean leadership and let slip by opportunity after opportunity to lead the people, and stopped His disciples from aggressively advancing the Messianic kingdom, Judas must have become increasingly confused and bitter. After all, he did believe in Jesus or he would not have remained with Him for so long.

The Two Betrayers

As Jesus failed to implement the Messianic kingdom Judas decided to take matters into his own hands. By betraying Jesus to the religious leaders of Judea (he appears able to approach them as an equal, suggesting that the priests and scribes knew him and considered him credible, perhaps because he was a Judean scribe) Judas thought he would force Jesus to overcome His strange inertia. Then the Master would set up His kingdom. The expectation was strong even among the other disciples. They had been arguing about their rank and position before the Last Supper (Luke 22:24-26). The mother of James and John had asked for official positions for them when Jesus became king (Matt. 20:20-24; Mark 10:35-40). Jesus had earlier promised that those who followed Him would be amply rewarded in this life (Matt. 19:28; Mark 10:28-30). One can only conclude that they expected Jesus to confront the Romans and other authorities when He went to the feast at Jerusalem.[10] Peter even expressed a willingness to die in battle for Him (Matt. 26:33; Mark 14:29-31; Luke 22:33-35).

Thus although he sought to engineer a confrontation between Jesus and His Judean opponents, Judas did not expect

Jesus to let Himself be taken captive. The disciple firmly expected his Master to resist. And the shock of the experience would remind Him what His real mission was. The 30 pieces of silver was a small amount for what he did, so Judas was not turning in his Master for money.[11] Judas tried to force Jesus to act as he thought the Messiah should. But he was not the only one who attempted to manipulate Christ. Peter had already done the same thing.

When Jesus told the disciples that He would go to Jerusalem to suffer and die at the hands of the religious leaders, "Peter took him aside and began to rebuke him, saying, 'God forbid it, Lord! This must never happen to you'" (Matt. 16:22). The disciple refused to accept the idea of Jesus dying on a cross. Like Judas, he believed that the national deliverer would vanquish Israel's enemies. That belief, though, accompanied a fierce loyalty to Christ. "But he [Jesus] turned and said to Peter, 'Get behind me, Satan! You are a stumbling block to me; for you are setting your mind not on divine things but on human things'" (verse 23). Peter was the unwitting voice of Satan's temptation to Jesus to abandon His mission on earth. Satan was using both Peter and Judas[12] to discourage and destroy.

Human beings can become tools of Satan while still believing that they are fiercely devoted to God. As the Temple police arrested Jesus, Peter drew his sword, attempting to defend his Master, not realizing that it was contrary to everything Jesus had come to earth to do. Peter considered himself completely dedicated to Christ. Yet events would soon demonstrate how weak that allegiance really was. He vowed that he would never deny Him (Matt. 26:35). But he would, as Jesus prophesied, disassociate himself from Christ three times before morning. And lest we condemn only him, the other disciples made the same vow. They denied Christ by fleeing for their lives.

The Saviour Who Does Not Give Up

At first glance it might seem that Jesus revealed the identity of His betrayer. In John 13:21 He declares, "Very truly, I tell you, one of you will betray me." One of the disciples—at Peter's prompting—asks who it would be (verses 24, 25). Jesus replies, "It is the one to whom I give this piece of bread when I have dipped it in the dish" and hands it to Judas (verse 26). D. J. Williams comments that "it seems likely from this Gospel that Judas was in the place of special honor at the Last Supper. The usual arrangement at such a meal was to have a series of couches, each accommodating three people, arranged in a U around the table. The host reclined in the center of the chief couch at the center of the curve of the U. The guests reclined on either side of him, leaning on their left elbow and eating with their right hand. The place of honor was to the left and, therefore, in a sense, behind the host." [13]

Judas makes his final decision to betray, and Jesus says to him, "Do quickly what you are going to do" (verse 27). But notice that the other disciples have no idea what is going on between Judas and their Master. They think that because Judas was their treasurer, Jesus was either directing him to buy what they needed for Passover or that he should donate something for the poor (verses 28, 29).

The disciple may be about to turn Jesus over to the Judean authorities, but Jesus refuses to expose him. He still loved him. Handing someone bread dipped in sauce at a meal was an ancient expression of honor and friendship. [14] "In normal circumstances the giving of the morsel was a mark of favor. Moreover, it would appear that Judas was in the place of honor since Jesus was able to hand him the piece of bread (John 13:26). We should take this portrayal of Jesus' action, then, as a sign of His friendship with Judas despite His knowledge of Judas' intentions. It was His last appeal to Judas to change his course. His words 'What you are going to do, do quickly' (John 13:27) were in effect a demand on Judas to make up his mind either to respond to Jesus' friendship or to betray him." [15]

On the other hand, Jesus clearly told Peter what the disciple would soon do. He knew that this disciple must be confronted with his weakness. Peter must be helped to face the fact of his own flaws. The impulsive disciple had to see his own nature and need before he could ask for and receive help. Jesus deals with each of us in the way that is best for us. It is our choice to accept or reject His working in our lives. Peter would respond to Christ's love because he let himself recognize and acknowledge his failings. Judas turned away from the Master's love because he considered it weakness on Christ's part.

He emotionally and spiritually pulled away from Jesus, as we see in Matthew 26:47-49. When Judas came with the mob he called Him "Rabbi" instead of "Lord." In the process he removed himself from the circle of disciples. But even then Jesus called him "friend" (verse 50), a word only Matthew uses and never in direct address to any other person. It appears twice elsewhere in parables (Matt. 20:13; 22:12). "In all cases the one addressed is committing an ungrateful action against the one who has been generous. Here it highlights the very important relationship of trust which exists between Jesus and Judas."[16]

The Decision to Be Saved or Lost

Judas took himself so far away from Jesus that he could never forgive himself or accept Jesus' forgiveness. In the hour of his self-imposed despair he saw no solution except suicide (Matt. 27:3-5; Acts 1:18). But Peter took advantage of his opportunity to repent. Forgiveness is hard for a person to accept, though. Jesus understood that Peter needed a concrete way to show his repentance. All human beings must have some method of demonstrating their sorrow and transformation. Thus Jesus repeated the miracle of the full fishing nets (John 21:4-11) to remind Peter of his original summons to discipleship (Luke 5:1-11). It enabled Peter to feel called again. Then, by repeating the question "Do you love me?" Christ signaled His acceptance of the repentant disciple (John 21:15-19). And because Peter's betrayal had left the man feeling alienated not only from Jesus but the disciples also, the Master conducted His reconciliation with Peter in their presence so they would know that Jesus still loved Peter despite what he had done. Peter's behavior had hurt the community of faith, and now Jesus brought healing and restoration to all.

Wooed or Seduced

As we have seen, Jesus held open His forgiveness and acceptance to Judas as long as he was able to respond—but the disciple rejected it. Pride and his own idea of what the Messiah should do and be drove him to spurn it. He was not predestined to betray Jesus to His enemies as some believe. The decision was his alone. Judas surrendered to his own weaknesses and refused Christ's offer of the Holy Spirit to transform him.

Peter, on the other hand, although he at first gave in to his flaws, finally chose to let Jesus be the Lord of his life. When Jesus warned Peter that he would betray Him, He told the disciple, "I have prayed for you that your own faith may not fail" (Luke 22:32). But if Peter did succumb to his fears and denied his relationship to Christ, that did not mean he was lost. The disciple could return if he repented. In fact, if he did, he could do wonderful things for his Master: "When once you have turned back, strengthen your brothers" (verse 32). Thus "Peter, from Galilee, finds his way to genuine repentance, whereas Judas, from Judea, in spite of his remorse exercises the final judgment upon himself." [17]

God woos our hearts. Satan attempts to seduce us. Which we respond to is our choice. The Holy Spirit does everything possible to help us, but the ultimate decision is ours alone. We can decide to be lost as Judas did, or follow the example of Peter and come to Christ.

---

[1] See Bruce J. Malina and Richard L. Rohrbaugh, *Social-Science Commentary on the Synoptic Gospels* (Minneapolis: Fortress Press, 1992), pp. 354-356.

[2] *Ibid.*, p. 168; *Social-Science Commentary on the Gospel of John* (Minneapolis: Fortress Press, 1998), pp. 44-46. Their assertion that present-day European Jews are mainly the descendants of Khazar converts may be questionable, but their other points are valid.

[3] Craig S. Keener, *The IVP Bible Background Commentary: New Testament* (Downers Grove, Ill.: InterVarsity Press, 1993), p. 252.

[4] Scholars have interpreted the term *Iscariot* in a number of ways, ranging from an indication that he belonged to a group of knife-wielding assassins, that he was a "false one" (from the Hebrew *sāqar*), "the one handing over" to Jesus' enemies, to someone from a village named Kerioth in Judea or elsewhere (*Anchor Bible Dictionary* [New York: Doubleday, 1992], vol. 3, pp. 1091, 1092). Other scholars have made additional suggestions (see, for example,

International Standard Bible Encyclopedia [Grand Rapids: Eerdmans, 1982], vol. 2, pp. 1151, 1152). D. J. Williams writes that Judas "is three times identified as the son of Simon (John 6:71; 13:2, 26). Since Simon is also called Iscariot, and Iscariot is further explained by the addition of *apo karyōtou* in some textual witnesses of John 6:71; 12:4; 13:2; 26 and 14:22, it would appear that Iscariot identifies Judas as 'a man (Heb. *is*) of Kerioth.' . . . Judas appears to have been the exception among the Twelve in not being a Galilean" (*Dictionary of Jesus and the Gospels* [Downers Grove, Ill.: InterVarsity Press, 1992], p. 406).

[5] Malina and Rohrbaugh, *Synoptic Gospels,* pp. 44, 45.

[6] Keener, p. 68.

[7] The Gospels tend to associate the scribes with Judea.

[8] *Anchor Bible Dictionary,* vol. 3, p. 1096.

[9] John Sanders, *The God Who Risks,* p. 99.

[10] *International Standard Bible Encyclopedia,* vol. 2, pp. 1152, 1153.

[11] *Ibid.,* p. 1152.

[12] Jesus never said anything to Judas similar to His rebuke to Peter. In fact, the Gospels do not have Judas falling under the influence of Satan until during the Last Supper (Luke 22:3).

[13] *Dictionary of Jesus and the Gospels,* p. 407.

[14] Keener, p. 298; George R. Beasley-Murray, *John,* Word Biblical Commentary (Waco, Tex.: Word Books, 1987), vol. 36, p. 238.

[15] *Dictionary of Jesus and the Gospels,* p. 408.

[16] *Anchor Bible Dictionary,* vol. 3, p. 1093.

[17] *Ibid.*

CHAPTER 3

Two Righteous Men

Ꙭ

How do you cope when your world seems to be coming to an end? For Noah it would be the destruction of a planet, and for Job it would involve the collapse of his personal world. Each survived only because of his trust in God and the strength and protection the Lord gave him. No person can make it alone, even in good times, as millions are discovering for themselves in today's increasingly fragmented society. But when trials and suffering threaten to overwhelm, the need for support from others becomes glaringly obvious. Even human help fails in the end. Only God can enable anyone to make it through the ultimate challenges.

Righteous Noah

The stories of both Noah and Job have their setting in the struggle between good and evil. We will look first at Noah. He lived in a world that had so rejected God that it was about to self-destruct. Humanity's every thought and action focused on evil (Gen. 6:5). Human violence and evil had reached the point that God could not let it go any further. The creation He had proclaimed "very good" (Gen. 1:31) had become "corrupt" (Gen. 6:11). Twice God declared that He was sorry that He had made humanity (verses 6, 7). What they had turned themselves into by their own choice "grieved him to his heart" (verse 6).

Many theologians construct a God out of philosophical speculation. They visualize a passive God aloof from His creation and free from any emotion. Only a God who never changes can, according to human philosophy, be perfect. To respond even emotionally to His creation would be to change, and for Him to change in any way would, by their definition, cause Him to be no longer perfect. They believe that a perfect being cannot change, because change is always for the worse.[1]

But God here agonizes over what has happened to His creation. Some English translations say He "repented" or "was sorry" that He had made humanity. "Can God change his mind?" Walter Brueggemann asks. "Can he abandon the world which he has so joyously created? . . . Many people hold a view of God as unchanging and indifferent to everything going on in the world, as though God were a plastic, fixed entity. But Israel's God is fully a person who hurts and celebrates, responds and acts in remarkable freedom. God is not captive of old resolves. God is as fresh and new in relation to creation as he calls us to be with him. He can change his mind, so that he can abandon what he made; and he can rescue that which he has condemned."[2]

The Lord interacts with His creation and can suffer from what happens to it. He took a risk when He created humanity, and when evil entered the picture the cosmic struggle began between Him and Satan. At this point in Genesis God despairs. It seems that the only solution is to terminate the whole experiment. But He doesn't—because of Noah. The patriarch "found favor in the sight of the Lord" (verse 8), and because of him God will not reject the new world but will become involved even more deeply with it, seeking to salvage it by saving Noah and his family.

"Noah was a righteous man, blameless in his generation; Noah walked with God" (verse 9). The Old Testament uses the word "righteous" to describe a person who avoids sin and does good to his or her neighbors.[3] "Blameless" implies wholeness or completeness, and the Septuagint (the first Greek translation of the Old Testament) applies the word to sacrificial animals. Only the blameless may dwell on God's holy hill (Ps. 15:1, 2), and it is the prerequisite for intimate fellowship with God. Scripture also employs both words to describe Job.[4] Noah also walked with God, a characteristic he shared with Enoch (Gen. 5:23, 24). The Bible frequently uses the imagery of "walking" to describe a whole way of life. The patriarch lived in obedience and relationship with God. The rest of humanity may have been corrupt, but God would rescue Noah and his family.

God tells Noah that He plans to destroy His creation with a flood (verse 17), but Noah will survive. He must construct an ark (verses 14-16) and enter it with his family and representative examples of the various kinds of living things (verses 18-20). The Lord said He would establish a protective covenant with Noah (verse 18).

Noah began building the ark. Most likely he proclaimed the world's coming destruction whenever he wasn't laboring on the vessel. The apostle Peter calls him "a herald of righteousness" (2 Peter 2:5). Jewish tradition in such works as the Sibylline Oracles and Jubilees portrayed Noah as preaching a call for repentance.[5] The construction of the ark itself was a testimony of God's warning. But as the years dragged by and those who had responded to his preaching died or drifted back into the world's corruption, Noah must have become discouraged. Did he wonder if he had misunderstood what God wanted him to do? Perhaps the Lord had not really asked him to build a boat on dry land in anticipation of an event that the world had never experienced before. Only his trust in God enabled him to endure the constant scoffing.

Peter, as did many other Jewish teachers of his era, saw the flood of Noah's time as a precursor of the world's final destruction (2 Peter 2:5).[6] Noah became the model for those who await Christ's return. Today God's people might not be constructing a physical ark, but all that we do should be a sermon to the world. Whether it be Bible studies with others, evangelistic sermons, living moral and spiritual lives in an increasingly corrupt world, educating our children to have faith in God—all this is our counterpart to Noah's work.

The people of Noah's world must have constantly challenged his belief in a coming deluge. Today's Noahs must also face skepticism and ridicule. We must, as perhaps he did, struggle with doubt and discouragement. Although we may have preached the Second Coming longer than Noah did the Flood, that does not make it any less real, or the final destruction any less sure. And

God promises that many more will respond to our preaching than to Noah's.

At last the day came when God told Noah and his family to board the ark (Gen. 7:1). The Flood then burst upon the earth. In Genesis 1 God created the world out of chaos and declared it good. But in Genesis 7 He "de-created" it because it had become evil. The description of the Flood follows in reverse order the events of Creation. Genesis 1:6-8 tells how God separated the waters above from the waters below. Genesis 7:11 mingles them again. Dry land emerges in Genesis 1:9, 10 and vanishes in Genesis 7:19, 20. The living things He created in Genesis 1:20-26 He blotted out in Genesis 7:21-23. The good creation that had become corrupt was no more. Only Noah and his family survived (verse 23).

Then God "remembered" Noah (Gen. 8:1). "Similarly, God 'remembered' Abraham after the destruction of Sodom (19:29); he 'remembered' Rachel (30:22), and he 'remembered' his covenant made in 9:15, 16, etc. Man is bidden not simply to 'remember' the past but the future (e.g., Isa 47:7; Eccl 11:8), which suggests that the word is more equivalent to 'think about' than to a concept of recall. . . . When God remembers, he acts, e.g., saving Lot, giving Rachel children, bringing Israel out of slavery (Exod 2:24; 6:5). This is the first time God is said to have remembered someone, and the passage is a paradigm of what that means in practice." [7]

The Lord now begins to re-create the earth, following the same sequence as in Genesis 1. A wind blows (Gen. 8:1; cf. Gen. 1:2), the fountains of the deep and the windows of heaven close (Gen. 8:2; cf. Gen. 1:6), the waters recede (Gen. 8:3; cf. Gen. 1:9, 10), and the dove returns with an olive leaf (Gen. 8:11; cf. Gen. 1:11, 12). Finally God permits the saved animals and human beings to leave the ark and be fruitful and multiply (Gen. 8:15-19; cf. Gen. 1:21-28). [8] (One wonders if the incident in Genesis 8:20-27 is a kind of counterpart to Genesis 3: people get into trouble over fruit, and God puts a curse on one of those involved.)

God took a risk when He created the world, and it disappointed Him. But He does not give up. He creates again. And He will re-create one final time. God's people await "the coming of the day of God, because of which the heavens will be set ablaze and dissolved, and the elements will melt with fire." "But, in accordance with his promise, we wait for new heavens and a new earth, where righteousness is at home" (2 Peter 3:12, 13). Revelation 21:1 foretells a new heaven and earth replacing the old ones.[9] God does not give up on His creation.

God Upheld the Ark

Noah's experience in the ark also models another principle of salvation. Many Christians, especially in North America, believe that they must be ready to take care of themselves during the last days. We saw this mentality behind some of the Y2K hysteria a few years ago. Believers in the rapture teaching assume that those still on earth after it takes place must endure the suffering of the tribulation largely through their own efforts. Some seek remote hideaways and stockpile weapons and supplies to make it through to the end. But the story of Noah shows that salvation in any form comes only from God. Yes, Noah built the ark, but it would not have survived the Flood without God's constant protection. No wooden boat, no matter how strongly constructed, could have floated unharmed in a global deluge. The salvation of Noah and his family came totally from God. Noah, whose name means "rest," rested in God's care until the ark "came to rest on the mountains of Ararat" (Gen. 8:4). As the storms raged around the ark, Noah must have been in constant awe of God's powers both to devastate and to save. He and his family could trust only in His promise to protect them. It is a trust that all of God's people must have.

"Have You Considered Job?"

Job was also a blameless and upright man (Job 1:1, 8), but his story takes a different course as he becomes, for a moment, the focus of the struggle between good and evil, God and Satan, that some call the great controversy.

Satan (as we saw previously, the name means "accuser" or "adversary") challenges God's evaluation of Job as blameless and upright (Job. 1:8). "Does Job fear God for nothing? Have you not put a fence around him and his house and all that he has, on every side? You have blessed the work of his hands, and his possessions have increased in the land. But stretch out your hand now, and touch all that he has, and he will curse you to your face" (verses 9-11).

Edwin M. Good sees Satan as so confident that Job will turn against God under pressure that he puts his own fate on the line. Good says that Satan "proposes that Yahweh 'touch' Job's possessions and goes on: 'If he doesn't curse you to your face . . .' (1:11). The statement is a self-curse that omits the result clause. The curse formula is 'If A happens (or does not happen), may B happen.' Usually the B clause is omitted (Job 31 presents a series of such curses, and in some, e.g., verses 7-8, 9-10, the B clause is present). According to Job 1:11, the Prosecutor[10] [Satan] is willing to call down a calamity upon himself. He proposes neither a test ('Let's see if he flunks') nor a wager. The Prosecutor puts his own welfare on the line: the present clause implies the continuation, 'May something awful happen to me!'"[11] Someday God will finish Satan's curse: "If Job does not curse you, may something terrible happen to me!" Revelation 20 describes that fate.

The accuser wants God to "touch" Job, but he is the one who does the actual destruction (Job 1:12). Tragedy after tragedy strikes the patriarch. Both "natural" and human-caused disasters wipe out Job's possessions and kill his household, both children and servants—in other words, the whole extended family except for him and his wife (verses 13-19).

When Job does not curse (verses 20-22), Satan demands a chance to increase the pressure (Job 2:1-5). He would break Job. God permits Satan to do his worst to the patriarch, short of taking his life (verses 6-8), but Job still refuses to turn against God even after a painful disease torments his body (verse 10). Then Job's friends come to "console and comfort him" (verse 11), but it seems that they play into Satan's hand and only increase the man's suffering (Job 4-31). Later Elihu joins the criticism of Job (Job 32-37). All their words inflict as much agony as Job's previous calamities.

While the destruction of family and material security was great, the most painful part of his suffering was that they represented the loss of every kind of support and self-identity life offers except for one. His economic world collapsed, his family was dead, his wife vented her grief against him (Job 2:9), his friends felt estranged from him (verses 11-13 and throughout the cycle of speeches in the rest of the book), and his own body failed him as he struggled with a debilitating disease. The religious philosophy that had until then sustained him intellectually now began to crumble under the attacks of his friends and his own questioning of all that he had once so confidently believed. Even his trust in God started to unravel. But in the end that was the one support that did not fail him. Though he suffered every imaginable kind of emotional, physical, and intellectual pain and even felt cut off from God, he still refused to let go of Him. Job might not understand why God was doing all this to him, but he would not abandon his loyalty and commitment to the Lord.

God Himself, in the person of the Son, would one day walk in Job's suffering footsteps. Christ would redeem human suffering, not by explaining it but by sharing it. As we noted earlier, to be able to explain evil would give it reason for its being. Saying that Job suffered because Satan sought to test the patriarch's loyalty to God makes what the accuser did seem almost necessary. But did Job's family and friends have to die just to prove his faith in God? In a similar manner we must be careful how we approach the subject of the cross. We must not reduce the meaning and horror of His death to little more than a legal transaction to pay for our salvation. It was infinitely more than that, and at the same time totally inexplicable and shocking. Throughout eternity we shall explore both its meaning and meaninglessness. The Crucifixion was terrible and should never have happened, yet the fact that it did is the most wonderful thing that ever took place in the universe.

Jesus, like Job, found Himself without this world's goods or power. His friends deserted Him, fleeing for their lives. And, like Job, He felt cut off from the Father—as we see when He cried out on the cross, "My God, my God, why have you forsaken me?" (Matt. 27:46). Christ's suffering was infinitely beyond that of Job, yet both endured for the same reason. Job clung to the memories of his earlier relationship with the Lord, and Christ held on to the Father's love even when it seemed withdrawn. Christ finished the journey that Job began so that someday nobody in the universe would ever have to walk it again.

The Power of the Creator

The two patriarchs responded to the destruction of their worlds in different ways. Noah obeyed God without apparent question, while Job struggled with doubt and anger. God directly involved Himself in Noah's world but remained mysterious and hidden to Job. While God did eventually speak to Job, He never explained what happened to him. Although both men were morally and spiritually righteous, the Lord protected one and let the other suffer without telling him why. Yet God vindicated them both in a questioning world.

God confirmed the truth of Noah's preaching when He sent the Flood. In a world that equated prosperity with God's blessing the Lord demonstrated Job's righteousness by restoring his wealth and bestowing a new family (Job 42:10-17). But these were still only temporary and but a foretaste of the final vindication. The world soon reverted to evil even in Noah's day. In time Job and his family died. Someone else inherited his wealth. The most important thing we can learn from their stories is not what happened but *what will yet happen.* The Lord will bring the struggle between good and evil to a final end. And the certainty of that end rests in the power of God as Creator.

As we have already seen, the Flood story of Genesis 8 parallels the Creation story of Genesis 1. But it also points to the re-creation promised in Revelation 21. Interestingly, in Revelation 14 the first of the three angels who proclaim the gospel to the whole world summons humanity to "worship him who made heaven and earth, the sea and the springs of water" (verse 7). It is a clear allusion to the Creation story and God's power as Creator. The God who created the world then re-created it after the Flood can re-create it yet a final time after evil is forever destroyed.

The book of Job is full of creation imagery. Job in his suffering calls for a reversal of Creation (Job 3). He wants everything to return to the dark chaos at the beginning. But God also uses His power in creation to defend Himself in His speech from the whirlwind (Job 38-40). The Lord asks Job if he can do the same things God can do in the natural world, emphasizing the deity's infinitely greater power. The Creator tells how He cares for the animals of His creation. If He cares for the beasts of the natural world, will He have less regard and concern for His human creation? Job might not understand what was happening to him, but he can trust in God's love and protection— even if it seems absent. God was constantly demonstrating it in the natural world.

Once we come to know the awesome God of Creation, we can rest in the assurance of His promise to vindicate all our suffering, all our service to Him in a hostile, sin-filled world. "See, I am coming soon; my reward is with me, to repay according to everyone's work" (Rev. 22:12). "Blessed are those who wash their robes, so that they will have the right to the tree of life and may enter the city by the gates" (verse 14).[12] The power of Him who can create and destroy worlds can erase the suffering and restore the lives of all who trust Him.

---

[1] John Sanders discusses systematic theology's concept of divine immutability and its relationship to the biblical evidence in *The God Who Risks*.

[2] Walter Brueggemann, *Genesis* (Atlanta: John Knox Press, 1982), p. 78. See John Sanders, *The God Who Risks*, especially pages 66-75, for a discussion of what the Bible means when it says that God "repents" of something.

[3] Gordon J. Wenham, *Genesis 1-15*, Word Biblical Commentary (Waco, Tex.: Word Books, 1987), vol. 1, p. 170.

[4] *Ibid.*, pp. 169, 170.

[5] C. Keener, *IVP Bible Background Commentary: New Testament*, p. 729.

[6] *Ibid.*, p. 718.

[7] Wenham, p. 184.

[8] Although God does not have to re-create day and night and the sun,

moon, and stars (His natural devices to measure time), He does mention them in Genesis 8:22.

[9] Could the sea that is "no more" be an allusion to the waters of Genesis 1 and their threat of returning chaos?

[10] The scenes in heaven in Job 1 and 2 are trial scenes, with Satan acting as the prosecuting attorney.

[11] *Harper's Bible Commentary,* p. 410.

[12] The tree of life and the river of life echo Genesis 1:9, 10.

CHAPTER 4

"And They Became One"
ન્ન

When God created Eve to be Adam's companion, God said, "I will make him a helper as his partner" (Gen. 2:18).[1] The inhabitants of the biblical world understood that a wife must be a helper to her husband. As we shall see throughout this book, people could survive only as they worked closely together. Wives, besides bearing and raising children, labored beside their husbands in the fields and among the flocks; raised, prepared, and cooked food; made clothing and all the other household goods they needed; and managed the extended household. Women did not sit at home as decorative objects or status symbols while their husbands earned their living for them. Couples either worked together as a team or they perished.

The biblical ideal of the wife's role appears in Proverbs 31:10-31. According to the poem of the virtuous or capable wife, she not only is spouse and mother (verses 11, 12, 28), but also supports her husband in public life (verse 23); sews (which was an economic necessity, not a hobby or pastime) (verses 13, 19); provides food for the family (verses 14, 15); buys and plants a vineyard (verse 16); sells merchandise (verses 15, 17, 18); helps the poor of the community (verse 20); clothes her family and dresses well herself (verses 21, 22); manufactures and sells clothing (verse 24); teaches (verse 26); and directs the work of the family (verse 27). Such a wife "does not eat the bread of idleness" (verse 27). For all her efforts she receives the praise of both her family (verse 28) and the community (verse 31).

The need for the whole family to work together kept husband and wife for all practical purposes as equals. But as urban life developed and some men became wealthier, wives who did less physical work outside the house became status symbols, and at the same time lost some of their equality with their husbands. They became more possession and less partner. No longer did they participate as actively in family decisions. Interestingly, a larger proportion of the Bible's stories about wives focuses on elite or higher class families.

As has always been the case throughout human history, wives could either be an asset to their husbands or a liability. They could give good advice or bad, help their husbands in life or destroy it. Priscilla was a coworker with Aquila in the church (Acts 18:26; Rom. 16:3; 1 Cor. 16:19), while Rebekah helped trick Isaac; Solomon's wives led him into paganism (1 Kings 11:4), and Jezebel filled Ahab's reign with evil. We will look at examples of both helpful and harmful wives.

Abigail and the Fool

When David fled from Saul's court he offered the local landowners protection of their flocks in exchange for food and other help. Nabal, whose name means "fool"[2] in Hebrew, lived up to the meaning of his name. During sheep-shearing season David sends a delegation to Nabal to ask for the traditional hospitality[3] and to establish a covenant. At the same time the men hint that it would not be good for Nabal to reject the offer (1 Sam. 25:4-8). The threefold repetition of "peace" and the statement that David's men have done no harm to Nabal's estate implies that he won't have any peace if he spurns the request (verse 6). David wants a good down payment on the bargain-to-be (verse 8). After all, it is a feast day, a time to share.

Nabal, however, cares only about his wealth. The rich man feels that he can do whatever he pleases. He neither fears nor respects anyone else.[4] Ignoring political and social reality (David has a powerful army and Saul is losing political control of the kingdom), Nabal dismisses David as nothing more than a runaway servant (verse 10).

Not only does Nabal's reply anger David, but the future king decides that he has to make an example of the arrogant landowner or he will lose all credibility with the rest of the people. If he doesn't deal with Nabal, other landowners would also refuse to aid David. David knows that he cannot survive in the struggle with Saul without such support. So he leads about 400 of his men on a raid against Nabal (verse 13).

Abigail, Nabal's wife, is not only beautiful but has the brains and common sense Nabal lacks (verse 3).[5] When she learns from one of her servants about the impending raid, she takes charge of the situation, determining to save her husband from himself. She has her servants load food for 600 men (probably from the feast for the sheep shearers) and starts out to intercept the warrior-king. Through diplomacy and charm she persuades him to call off the attack (verses 23-35).

Bowing, apologizing, and presenting herself as David's servant, she first uses gentle humor to defuse the crisis by playing with the meaning of her husband's name (verse 25). Then she points out that God has been with David and that the Lord has so far restrained him from bloodguilt against Nabal or others (verse 26). David should, she softly suggests, let God fight his battles (verses 28-30). If he will do that, he will not suffer grief or guilt from any rash actions (verse 31). She also gives him a way of saving face in front of his men and the larger community. He can explain his calling off the attack by making her, instead of Nabal, the beneficiary of his new decision.[6] Nabal's wife speaks to "my lord" (verses 28, 29, 31) as to a future king. And she concludes, "When the Lord has dealt well with my lord, then remember your servant" (verse 31).[7]

David thanks her for her good sense and for stopping an armed raid that could have been disastrous in many ways. Perhaps he now realizes that instead of making Nabal an example, he might have alienated many of those whose support he needs to become king. He blesses God who sent Abigail to him (verse 32), her good sense (verse 33), and finally Abigail herself (verse 33). "David is a free man, free of vengeance—thanks to Abigail. She has saved his life and his future."[8]

Abigail also accomplished her goal of saving Nabal's life,

whether he deserved it or not. But all that she did for him was of no avail. He was at home drunk, feeling like a "king" (verse 36), unaware that he had escaped death by a real king. When he became sober enough to understand what she had done, "his heart died within him" (verse 37). Ten days later he was physically dead (verse 38).

Wives in the Book of Esther

The book of Esther presents an interesting series of wives. The first is Vashti. As the book opens, King Ahasuerus[9] stages a series of banquets (Esther 1). The first banquet, lasting for 180 days, entertains officials from throughout the empire (verses 1-4). Then he arranges a seven-day feast for the citadel of Susa (verse 5). The biblical writer depicts a scene of ostentatious display and conspicuous consumption (verses 6, 7). On the seventh day, while "merry with wine" (verse 10),[10] the king orders Vashti the queen to display her beauty.

He has already flaunted the splendor and power of empire throughout the previous celebration, and now he wants to exhibit Vashti. The account is not clear as to exactly what the king had in mind, but many commentators feel that he intended to display her in a degrading way. Vashti refuses to come to the banquet, even though Ahasuerus dispatches seven eunuchs to convey his command and bring her (verses 10-12). If nothing else, she does not want to be leered at by a bunch of drunken men and treated as some kind of prize possession. She will not cater to the questionable whims of a drunken ruler even though it costs her position and sends her into exile (verse 19). As Frederic Bush observes: "Vashti evidences the only element of decorum and decency in this world of opulence and excess."[11]

Her response angers the king (verse 12), but he does not know what to do about it. Somehow he has to save face. Raising a domestic squabble to an affair of state instead of dealing with it privately and quietly, he consults his counselors (verses 13, 14). They hysterically reply that her behavior threatens the stability of the whole empire. "Not only has Queen Vashti done wrong to the king, but also to all the officials and all the peoples who are in all the provinces of King Ahasuerus. For this deed of the queen will be made known to all women, causing them to look with contempt on their husbands, since they will say, 'King Ahasuerus commanded Queen Vashti to be brought before him, and she did not come.' That very day the noble ladies of Persia and Media who have heard of the queen's behavior will rebel against the king's officials, and there will be no end of contempt and wrath!" (verses 16-18).

The counselors decree what Vashti has already decided: "never again to come before King Ahasuerus" (verse 19). The king must choose another queen. (Perhaps they fear what she might do to them if she ever gets into the king's good graces again.) Although the counselors worry that the women of the realm might hear what Vashti did, by deposing her and passing a law that wives must honor their husbands (verses 20-22) they unwittingly ensure that everyone will learn what happened. And the book goes on to reveal a king totally guided by the advice of his next wife, Esther. Only she will be able to save him from the disastrous decree against the Jews.

Ahasuerus soon involves the Persian Empire in a costly war against the Greeks. Next, the edict that Haman tricks him into signing threatens to plunge the empire into civil war. Archaeological evidence suggests that the Jewish exiles had become a prosperous part of the Babylonian and Persian empires. Persia would pay a terrible price if the government tried to wipe them out. Besides the bloodshed, it would have ruined a significant part of the national economy—the Jewish merchants and artisans. In addition, such genocide would have demoralized society.

Esther 3:15 tells us that word of the edict threw the city of Susa into confusion. Frederic Bush interprets the statement as implying empathy on the part of the general population toward the predicament of the Jewish community.[12] The inhabitants of Susa could not understand why their king could do such a thing toward their neighbors, people they respected. As Levenson observes: "It may be that the Susan Gentiles were severely distressed at the thought that their streets would flow with the blood of the Jews who had been living peacefully in their midst." [13] It raised disturbing questions about their national leadership. Who would be the next victims?

The book of Esther depicts Ahasuerus as somewhat weak-willed and acting without thought beforehand. With God's help Esther guides the king through a resolution of the crisis. The king believes that he is the one making the decisions, but she is actually the one in control. The Persian men wanted honor from their wives (Esther 1:20). Esther, however, is the one that truly deserves honor.

Haman's Wife

But Esther is not the only example of reversal of the Persian leadership's desire that the men be masters of their households (verses 16-22). Haman, at first in euphoria at attending Esther's banquet for the king, plummets into depression and fury when he spots Mordecai, who refuses to bow to him (Esther 5:9). When he arrives home he tries to cheer himself up by bragging to Zeresh, his wife, about his wealth, the number of his sons, his honors from the king, and his presence with the queen at Esther's private banquet (verses 10-12). "Yet all this does me no good," he whines in despair, "so long as I see the Jew Mordecai standing at the king's gate" (verse 13). Zeresh[14] urges him to build a gallows for Mordecai. "This advice pleased Haman" (verse 14).[15] But he does not know that by listening to her he has started a series of events that will seal his fate and cost Zeresh her sons.

The next day, when Haman comes home to report to her and his friends his humiliation at having to honor Mordecai, she announces that he is doomed and will not prevail if Mordecai is indeed Jewish (Esther 6:13). She has destroyed her husband. Levenson suggests that Zeresh and the friends know the biblical prediction in Numbers 24:15-19 of Israel's triumph and Amalek's demise (verse 20). They interpret what Haman has just gone through as the first stage of the prophecies' fulfillment in their own time.[16] Even as they stand talking, the king's eunuchs arrive and hustle Haman off to Esther's second banquet and his fate (Esther 6:14)—a fate that Zeresh's advice worsened.

Pilate's Wife

In the New Testament we find another wife who tried to advise her husband what he should do. Unlike Zeresh's suggestion, it was good counsel, but this husband ignored his wife—to his great tragedy.

As the Roman governor Pilate debated what to do about Jesus, his wife sent him a message. "Have nothing to do with that innocent man," she urged him,[17] "for today I have suffered a great deal because of a dream about him" (Matt. 27:19). All ancient cultures in the Near East considered dreams as often revealing messages from supernatural sources.[18] Some have suggested that the wife was a convert[19] of Christ's, but Donald A. Hagner points out that Matthew uses the phrase "in a dream" elsewhere only for divine revelation (see Matt. 1:20; 2:12, 13, 19, 22).[20] The dream prompted her to refer to Jesus as "that righteous man."[21]

The warning from his wife only reinforced Pilate's impression that Jesus was innocent. The Roman official saw that the Jewish religious leaders were willing to do anything to destroy Christ. Pilate knew that Jesus was not guilty of the charge brought against Him. Although the governor probably had perverted justice himself, the travesty he witnessed in his courtroom still disturbed him. But other interests soon overwhelmed any remaining sense of justice he retained.

History records a Roman tradition of long standing that regarded provincial administration as an opportunity to become wealthy[22] and retire in luxury. Although by Pilate's time provincial governors received a salary instead of having to support themselves, there was still the temptation to accumulate as much wealth as quickly as possible. Some of the governors accepted bribes or extorted and defrauded the people they ruled. Although Palestine was a difficult province to administer, Pilate was fairly competent and lasted longer than his successors.[23] Still, he had some difficult relationships with the people of Palestine. Judea had never been conquered, only annexed, and the Jews bitterly resented the Roman occupation.[24] It was possible for the people of a province to get their governor recalled to Rome, and Pilate did not want to risk that.

Several times Pilate tried to free Jesus. But when the Jerusalem religious leadership shouted, "If you release this man, you are no friend of the emperor" (John 19:12), he capitulated. The threat alluded to a charge of *maiesta minuta,* neglect of state security. Such investigations were frequent during the period.[25] (In fact, Pilate would later have to go to Rome to face such an imperial interrogation. The Roman authorities expected an official to commit suicide if found guilty, which some evidence suggests Pilate may have done.)[26] Although he tried to reduce his responsibility for Jesus' death by the symbolic washing of his hands (Matt. 27:24),[27] he ignored even the good sense of his own wife.[28]

Not all men were fortunate to have wives of constant principle, good sense, or intelligence. Wives could get their husbands into trouble—a sad fact that goes back to the very beginning of human history. We have already looked at the example of Zeresh, and will briefly consider two more.

Sin began to spread through the world when a husband went along with his wife's wrong decision.

Take, Eat, and See

Eve ate from the tree of the knowledge of good and evil because she thought it would make her "wise" (Gen. 3:6). The serpent had told her that the fruit would make her "like God, knowing good and evil" (verse 5). Strangely, she did not believe God's warning about what would happen if she ate the forbidden fruit, yet she craved His attributes. She "took" and "ate" (verse 6). Wanting Adam, "who was with her" (verse 6), to join her quest to be a god, she gave him some of the fruit, and he ate too. Scripture has Adam remaining silent during the incident, an important point in the terse biblical style in which every word has significance. Eve's husband does not protest what she does. He goes along willingly, a fact that Paul alluded to when he wrote that Adam was not deceived (1 Tim. 2:14). Adam understood the full significance of his act of disobedience.

The serpent was partly right in what he told Eve. She *did* gain new knowledge. The woman and her husband now knew guilt, shame, fear, and a host of other things that they suddenly realized would have been better never to have learned. The couple became aware that they were "naked." Nakedness in the Bible means far more than being unclothed. The biblical symbol suggests weakness, neediness, helplessness (Deut. 28:48; Job 1:21; Isa. 58:7). Adam and Eve had been unaware of their total dependence on God. Now they knew, but in the act of acquiring that understanding they had destroyed themselves. Eve had gained new knowledge—and, to her horror, wished that she hadn't. The "knowledge of good and evil" is, as the serpent had hinted, something appropriate only to divinity, not to created, finite beings. "Ironically, what the man and woman discover is not that they are gods but that they are naked—weak, vulnerable, and helpless, having rejected their dependence upon God." [29]

The human race would have to live with the fatal consequences of that knowledge until Someone else said, "Take, eat" (Matt. 26:26). Jesus would turn these two verbs from precursors of death to a foretaste of salvation. [30]

Sarah

Eve wanted to be a god when she got her husband into trouble, but Sarah just longed to be a mother. Motherhood formed a large part of a woman's self-identity in the ancient world. A childless woman considered herself incomplete and even punished by God. A number of ancient cultures accepted the custom of substitute childbearing, and Sarah seized on such a concept to deal with her childlessness. Ancient society regarded slave women as legal extensions of their female owners. As one of her household duties Hagar could conceive children for Sarah. [31] She pressured her husband, " 'You see that the Lord has prevented me from bearing children; go in to my slave-girl; it may be that I shall obtain children by her.' And Abram listened to the voice of Sarai" (Gen. 16:2). Instead of the voice of God, Abraham listened to that of his wife.

But when Ishmael was born, Sarah discovered that she was still not happy—that she still craved her own child. To add to her misery, Hagar "looked with contempt on her mistress" (verse 4), perhaps from the feeling that she was a real woman since she could have a child and Sarah couldn't. Sarah then focused her hurt and disappointment on her husband. "May the Lord judge between you and me!" (verse 5) she exploded at him. But he had done only what she told him to do.

By trying to obtain children through Hagar, Sarah showed, like Eve, her lack of trust and belief in God. God had promised Sarah's husband a child, and she had been determined to make it come to pass one way or another. Her desire for a child became all-consuming—like Eve's desire to be as God—and it came between her and God. In addition, she threatened her husband's trust in God. As Brueggemann observes, Abraham's son Ishmael "is a temptation for Abraham to trust in the fruit of his own work rather than in [God's] promise (cf. 17:18). . . . [The apostle] Paul has seen correctly that . . . Hagar and Ishmael function as an alternative to the promise. They are visible evidence that in the short run, initiative can be taken from God and things will be better."[32]

Because Abraham listened to his wife at the wrong time and let her attempt to solve her longing for a child block God's promise, dissension tore apart his family, and eventually he lost his son Ishmael. The Lord had to send the lad away to help Abraham learn to trust God instead of himself and his actions.

Job's Wife

Abraham did what Sarah urged him at least partly out of his recognition of her overwhelming desire to have a child. It can be difficult to deny something that a spouse wants so intensely. Adam went along with Eve's desire for godlike powers. But Job said no to his wife's desperate request.

Job's wife is an enigmatic figure in some ways, but we can

understand some of the feelings that drove her. A string of disasters has killed their children and servants—their extended family—and destroyed their possessions, their source of survival in a harsh world. Everything that makes life meaningful—even possible—is now gone. Job and his wife live in a culture that sees everything that happens as a direct act of God. From their perspective God is punishing them. How much more can they take? From the depths of her grief and despair the wife comes to Job and demands, "Do you still persist in your integrity? Curse God, and die" (Job 2:9).

The original language actually says, "Bless God, and die." The Hebrew *barak* is ambiguous in this section of Job, sometimes standing for its usual meaning of "bless," other times implying "curse." [33] Clearly, though, she is urging Job to tell God to take his life and get the cruel punishment over with.

Through the centuries commentators have often seen and portrayed Job's wife as a villain, or at least a shrew. Her statement shocks us. Or does she have pity on her intensely suffering husband and beg him to accept the only escape she can see from a terrible situation? We forget that she is also enduring overwhelming grief. Such grief can drive any of us to echo Satan's doubts and magnify the suffering that sin causes. All of us have had loved ones inflict such pain on us—and we have done it to them.

"You speak as any foolish woman would speak," Job replies. "Shall we receive the good at the hand of God, and not receive the bad?" (verse 10). Job may have answered harshly to his wife, but it could also be that he may have sensed that he had to stop her plunge into despair. He could not allow her to continue on in self-destructive grief. Abraham gave what Sarah wanted at the moment, and it led to disaster. Job's wife wanted an end to suffering, and he could not let his wife add to their own immense tragedy. Beyond that, he had a faith that would, despite its struggle, sustain him in the end. Perhaps it ultimately strengthened her.

---

[1] Literally "a help as opposite him" or "corresponding to him" (Derek Kidner, *Genesis: An Introduction and Commentary* [Downers Grove, Ill.:

InterVarsity Press, 1967], p. 65).

[2] Probably a deliberate distortion of his real name (Joyce G. Baldwin, *1 & 2 Samuel: An Introduction and Commentary* [Leicester, Eng.: InterVarsity Press, 1988], p. 147).

[3] Christine D. Pohl, *Making Room: Recovering Hospitality as a Christian Tradition* (Grand Rapids: Eerdmans, 1999), p. 26.

[4] Walter Brueggemann, *First and Second Samuel* (Louisville: John Knox Press, 1990), p. 175.

[5] Scripture uses the same word "beautiful" *(yph)* of both David and Abigail (*ibid.*, p. 176).

[6] *Harper's Bible Commentary*, p. 283.

[7] Her appeal is for herself. And David grasps it. As soon as he learns of Nabal's death he begins wooing her. She responds quickly (1 Sam. 25:39-42).

[8] Brueggemann, *First and Second Samuel*, p 180.

[9] Commentators widely see Ahasuerus as Xerxes I (Frederic W. Bush, *Ruth, Esther*, Word Biblical Commentary [Dallas: Word Books, 1996], vol. 9, p. 345; Jon D. Levenson, *Esther: A Commentary* [Louisville: Westminster John Knox, 1997], p. 43).

[10] In the Bible a reference to intoxication seems to be a harbinger of doom. See, for example, 1 Samuel 25:36; 2 Samuel 13:28; and Daniel 5:2.

[11] Bush, p. 315.

[12] *Ibid.*, p. 383.

[13] Levenson, p. 77.

[14] The Hebrew word order of Esther 5:14 makes her the main spokesperson (Bush, p. 418).

[15] Note that the phrase about the idea pleasing him appears in both Esther 1:21 and 5:14, tying the two passages together and pointing out the irony of Haman being told what to do by his wife.

[16] Levenson, p. 99.

[17] It was only fairly recently that Rome had allowed its governors to take their wives with them to the provinces they administered. Although Roman culture did not approve of women taking active roles in public, it did allow them to influence their husbands privately, as Pilate's wife was now doing (Keener, *IVP Bible Background Commentary: New Testament*, p. 126).

[18] *Ibid.*

[19] As Origen claimed (*International Standard Bible Encyclopedia*, vol. 3, p. 869).

[20] Donald A. Hagner, *Matthew 14-28*, Word Biblical Commentary (Dallas: Word Books, 1995), vol. 33b, p. 823.

[21] *Ibid.*

[22] Lesley Adkins and Roy A. Adkins, *Handbook to Life in Ancient Rome* (New York: Oxford University Press, 1994), p. 44.

[23] *Anchor Bible Dictionary*, vol. 5, p. 398.

[24] *International Standard Bible Encyclopedia*, vol. 3, p. 868.

[25] Pilate's patron in Rome, Sejanus, was executed for treason in A.D. 31. For Pilate to ignore a pretender to kingship would have raised questions about his own allegiance. See Peter Richardson, *Herod: King of the Jews and Friend of the*

Romans (Columbia, South Carolina: University of South Carolina Press, 1996), p. 312.

[26] *Ibid.*, p. 869.

[27] See Hagner (pp. 826, 827) for the background of the custom.

[28] Strangely, the Ethiopian Coptic church eventually canonized Pilate as a saint (*Anchor Bible Dictionary,* vol. 5, p. 400).

[29] *Harper's Bible Commentary,* p. 88.

[30] Kidner, p. 68.

[31] John H. Walton and Victor H. Matthews, *IVP Bible Background Commentary: Genesis-Deuteronomy* (Downers Grove, Ill.: InterVarsity Press, 1997), p. 42.

[32] Brueggemann, *Genesis,* p. 152.

[33] *Harper's Bible Commentary,* p. 410.

CHAPTER 5

The Coat of Many Troubles

ॐ

The story of Joseph is an important one in the Bible. Scholars see it as a pattern for at least two other biblical narratives: the book of Esther[1] and the tragic story of David's daughter Tamar in 2 Samuel 13.[2] Preachers often focus on just two aspects of the Joseph story—how he resisted sexual temptation and how God worked through him to deliver his family. But the Joseph cycle of stories is also of how God matured an impetuous young man who had grown up in a highly dysfunctional family. God did save Joseph's family, but He worked through circumstances shaped by human will and choice as much as by divine guidance. And besides maturing Joseph, God brought divine healing to the rest of Jacob's family.

Jacob's Second Family

Joseph's father Jacob had always loved Rachel more than Leah, and this love continued to manifest itself even after her death. Jacob displayed obvious favoritism toward Rachel's children, Joseph and Benjamin. We first see Joseph as a 17-year-old shepherd helping some of his half brothers, the sons of Bilhah and Zilpah. Apparently they did something that disturbed Joseph, and he reported it to his father (Gen. 37:3). The story does not elaborate on what they did. The author is interested only in Joseph's behavior. Although in his time Joseph would have been a fully mature adult, he was acting more like a tattling child. The biblical world was obsessed with honor and shame.[3] Joseph's report shamed the brothers in their father's eyes. In addition, Jacob's wives had fought each other through their servants. Now Joseph perpetuated that discord by getting the sons

51

of the handmaidens into trouble. The favored son drove still another wedge between the members of his family.

Jacob doted on Joseph because "he was the son of his old age" (verse 3). To show his favoritism the father had "a long robe with sleeves" made for him. Traditional translations have rendered it as a coat of many colors. Walton and Matthews observe that while the coat may have been colorful, it was the material, fine weave, and length that made it valuable. We may get a hint of what the coat looked like from depictions of well-dressed Canaanites in Egyptian tomb paintings. They wore long-sleeved embroidered garments with a fringed scarf extending diagonally from waist to knee.[4] The term for robe in 2 Samuel 13:18 refers to a royal garment. Jacob clearly intended his gift to represent authority as well as favor. Yet Joseph was the next to youngest son in a culture that ranked the role and honor of sons by their birth order.

The robe not only was an indication that Jacob favored Joseph over his other sons; it slapped them in the face by ignoring all they understood about their place in the family. The father had earlier turned his family upside down by trying to reverse birth order and birthright. Now he was doing it again with his own sons. Jacob was still destroying family relationships. The Bible does not depict the brothers only as villains or stereotypes of evil. As much victim as Joseph soon would be, they recognized arbitrary love when they saw it, and it understandably evoked their hatred.[5] Since they could not do anything about their father, they vented their anger on the more loved son. The brothers found themselves caught between Joseph and Jacob. Their frustration eventually left them unable even to carry on a peaceful conversation with Joseph (Gen. 37:4).

The opening verses of the Joseph story depict a family destroying itself. The author reinforces this fact by placing the brothers' hatred of Joseph "against a background of relational and familial language: 'son(s)' occurs five times, 'father' four times, and 'brothers' three times."[6] Furthermore, none of them are free from guilt. Jacob flaunts his favoritism, Joseph stirs up family strife by reporting on his brothers, and the brothers give in to their hatred.[7]

Then Joseph further antagonizes them by describing two dreams he has had. In the first he and his brothers are binding sheaves of grain in the field. The sheaves are bundles of stalks quickly tied together and laid on the ground. But his bundle stands up, and those prepared by the other brothers gather around it and bow down (verses 5-7). The listening brothers instantly recognize the dream's implication. Such dreams of a rise to power were a standard motif in the ancient Near East. For example, hundreds of years earlier Sargon, king of Akkad, had had such a dream of his eventual assumption of rulership.[8] In Egypt one pharaoh claimed to have had a dream in which the Sphinx told him that he would unexpectedly become king. Joseph's brothers could in no way misinterpret what he was saying. Their younger brother was announcing that he would have authority over them. Again he was violating the ancient principle that sons had priority by order of birth.

Dreams Into Nightmares

To compound his audacity and insult, Joseph describes a second dream[9] in which the sun, moon, and 11 stars bow down to him (verse 9). "What kind of dream is this that you have had?" Jacob demands. "Shall we indeed come, I and your mother[10] and your brothers, and bow to the ground before you?" (verse 10). His brothers' jealousy only worsens.

God gave the dreams, but each member of the family, including Joseph, chose how they would respond to them. Joseph was too immature and self-centered to realize what presenting the dreams would do to his family. The brothers reacted as if the dreams were fuel tossed into the furnace of their hatred and rage. They did not even bother to speak to him. Only the father seemed to be open to the dreams as he "kept the matter in mind" (verse 11). Perhaps Jacob had learned "by now, as his sons had not, to allow for God's hand in affairs, and for His right of choice among men."[11] After all, he had seen what happens when one tries to take charge of God's plans.

Would God have worked the dreams out in ways other than

He did if Joseph and the others had made different choices? We can never know for sure, but John Sanders points out that at least one aspect of the dream was never fulfilled. The detail about Joseph's father and "mother" was conditional, because it never happened.[12] Both Rachel (Gen. 35:16-20) and Leah (Gen. 49:31) died in Canaan, and the biblical account never mentions Jacob bowing to Joseph. It is possible that Joseph's family could have avoided much pain and tragedy in the following years by following different courses. At least, all bear guilt and responsibility for how they responded to one another.

In many ways Joseph lived a moral life as a young person. He could not have later resisted the temptations of Egypt otherwise. But one can be highly moral and yet immature at the same time. Joseph had much to learn. Through the dreams God was indicating that He had great plans for Joseph. But the young man could not fulfill them until he had grown and matured in character.

The Encounter in Dothan

The brothers take the family flocks toward the north, to Shechem (Gen. 37:12). Jacob sends Joseph to "see if it is well" with them (verse 14). The Hebrew word translated "well" here is *shalom*, "peace." But Joseph will find no peace when he meets his brothers. Reaching Shechem, he discovers the brothers gone and begins wandering across the field where they should have been (verses 14, 15). A man asks him whom he is looking for. Joseph explains that he has come to see his brothers and asks where they might be pasturing their flocks now (verse 16). The stranger replies that he heard them talking about going to Dothan (verse 17).

Much is going on in this seemingly simple incident that escapes the attention of the modern reader, because few of us live in a pastoral world. The ancient reader would have quickly recognized something wrong. The brothers had no right to move the flocks.

Vegetation and water were (and are) scarce in Palestine, and herds could not remain long in any one place before they exhausted one or both. Usually as the wetter winter season turned into the dry summer, herders would first graze their flocks in harvested fields, then take them both north and to higher elevations, where enough vegetation still remained. Springs and wells would run dry, also forcing the herds to move on. But herders could not graze their flocks just anywhere. All the land suitable for pasture already belonged to someone. Farmers did not want flocks destroying their unharvested crops or depleting their water sources. Besides, too many flocks in one place for too long a time could strip the land bare, causing erosion. Tension always existed between the landowners and wandering pastoralists such as Jacob and his family. To further complicate matters, Jacob and his household were resident aliens in a land of limited and already strained resources. They were outsiders in a closely knit world. To survive, Jacob and his clan had to be willing to live by the rules set by the permanent inhabitants of the land.[13]

Sheepherders had to pay for the right to graze another person's land. It required careful and extensive negotiations, as we see in such passages as Genesis 21:22-33.[14] Pastoralists had to arrange for grazing rights before the start of the grazing season in any one spot. Only the head of the family or his representative could make such a treaty. A herdsman could not move his flocks at will.

Yet the brothers had done exactly that. Jacob had expected them to be at Shechem, because he had negotiated the treaty with the local landowners there. He knew nothing about grazing rights anywhere else. When the brothers shifted the flocks to Dothan, they had usurped Jacob's cultural role as negotiator and treaty maker. Only he had the authority to move the flocks, and only after he had established a treaty with the owners of the new pasture site. Sons in the biblical world could not make such decisions on their own as long as their fathers were still alive or if they had not given them authority to negotiate for them. The fact that Joseph had to hunt for his brothers shows that neither he nor Jacob knew anything about their transferring to Dothan. Jacob had not given permission to go anywhere else. The brothers had made the decision themselves. In their culture they were acting as if their father were already dead. Perhaps their frustration and anger at how Jacob treated them had destroyed their respect for him. More likely they were just behaving as their father had done all his life. Jacob had deceived his father; now his sons were deceiving him.

When the brothers spotted Joseph approaching them, all the resentment at him and their father burst into the flames of murder. If they could kill the dreamer, it would also destroy the dreams. With Joseph dead they would never have to worry about bowing down to him (verses 18-21). He would stop running their lives, turning everything upside down. Could the final spark that ignited their rage have been the fear that Joseph would report to their father their decision to move the flocks? They had had enough shame. Jacob had tricked his father with an animal skin. They would lie to him with the aid of a bloodstained robe. Their father had honored Joseph with the garment. Now they would dishonor him with that same piece of clothing. A gift of warped love had turned into a symbol of cruel hatred.

Joseph in Potiphar's House

Sermons and devotional writings have turned Potiphar's wife into little more than a symbol of pure evil and sexual lust, and Joseph into a stereotyped example of unsullied virtue. But both were real, complex human beings. Life is never so simplistic, so black and white. Could there have been more than just sexual desire behind her attempted seduction? What does the incident have to say to those of us who have to make decisions in a complex and often ambiguous world? And could these additional issues teach us something about what God hoped Joseph would learn from being allowed to go through such an experience?

The ancient world, including Egypt, divided reality into two spheres: home, and the world beyond it. In many ways they were two parallel societies. Men were responsible for the one outside the home, and women took care of the social world inside it. We must not view these dual worlds through the imaginary stereotypes of 1950s American television programs in which the wife stayed at home to cook, clean, and raise children while the husband went off to the office or factory to earn a living for the whole family. Rather, the household was for all practical purposes a complete economy in itself, requiring complex managerial and technical skills to operate it.

Ancient families did not go out and buy food, clothing, or whatever they needed. They had to raise or make almost everything. And women did almost all of this work. "Considerable expertise—planning, skill, experience, and technological knowledge—was necessary for the performance of a woman's tasks, many of which involved precise chemical and physical processes." [15] Carol Meyers observes that around the home and farm "female tasks required a higher degree of expertise, judgment, and skill than did male tasks." [16] It takes as much executive skill and insight to manage a household as it does a business or government.

Today modern Western society sees many advantages for both genders participating in each sphere of life, but the ancient world preferred to keep them separate, and Egypt was no exception. Joyce Tyldesley states that in ancient Egypt "the married woman's most coveted title of Mistress of the House was a constant reminder of her principal wifely duty: to ensure the smooth day-to-day running of her husband's home. It seems very unlikely that either sex would ever have dreamed of questioning the inevitability of this division of labour. Males and females were understood by all to be different types of people destined to live very different lives, and an upsetting of this natural order would clearly have been wrong." [17]

When Potiphar put Joseph in charge of his household, he placed his slave in a woman's role. Usually we think of Joseph's assignment from the perspective of a modern business manager. But the household was the wife's domain and responsibility. While the husband was the theoretical head of the household, the wife or dominant woman (such as a mother-in-law or sister-in-law) held the actual power. Joseph specifically states to Potiphar's wife that his master "is not greater in this house than I am" (Gen. 39:9). They were equals in the household; thus the wife had two men theoretically over her. The difference between them was that she was Potiphar's wife, not his, and he competed with her for authority in her own household. From any perspective Joseph had a most unusual role in Egyptian society.

Why would Potiphar go against cultural custom? Perhaps we can suggest two reasons—one on the human level and the other on the divine. The latter Joseph alluded to when he told his brothers that not they but God had sent him to Egypt (Gen. 45:8).

As for the human motivation on Potiphar's part, we first need to consider why he kept Joseph in prison after the wife accused the slave of attempted rape. Until fairly recently in human history prisons were just holding places until the convicted criminal was executed, forced to pay a fine, sold into slavery, or punished in some other way. Prison was not a long-term punishment. Yet Potiphar confined Joseph there for a number of years. It was as if the Egyptian official did not know what to do with his Hebrew slave.

Could he in the first place have put Joseph in charge of his household—traditionally a woman's role—because of some problem between him and his wife? Did she then, as Joseph's brothers had earlier when they found themselves caught between Joseph and their father, seek revenge? Yes, Joseph was good-looking, but was the really irresistible attraction that by seducing him she would be mocking and dishonoring the husband who had removed her from her rightful place? She could enjoy the slave's physical charms and also know that she had made a fool of the man who had usurped her role in life. And did Potiphar hesitate to execute Joseph for rape or refrain from selling him elsewhere because he sensed the young man's innocence? Did he guess that his wife had initiated the encounter because of their strained relationship? Had his plan backfired and made him feel guilty because of the harm it brought Joseph? We can only speculate.

God protected Joseph, but divine providence usually works through human action and motivation, as we see throughout this story. Clearly Potiphar did not fully believe his wife when she came to him with Joseph's garment (Jacob's family constantly seem to be getting into trouble because of something they wear).[18] Walton and Matthews suggest that Potiphar's choice of prison did indeed indicate that he understood the nature of the encounter between his servant and his wife. "Rather than being executed for rape . . . Joseph was put into a royal prison holding political prisoners. This may have been a bit more comfortable (as prisons go), but more importantly it will put him into contact with members of Pharaoh's court (Gen. 40:1-23)."[19] It is almost as if Potiphar had to do something to protect his honor, but he wanted the punishment as mild as possible.

From a divine perspective, it was as if God knew that by fulfilling a woman's duties Joseph would become a better man. To be a good ruler he must first become a faithful servant. Men might get away with being incompetent administrators, but a family starved if a woman fell down on her job. Women took care of the household, the basic unit of ancient culture. They were the underpinning of society. What better training could Joseph get? As he prospered in Potiphar's household, God was preparing him for service in Pharaoh's household and the nation of Egypt.

If Joseph did find himself caught between Potiphar and his wife, it echoes the experience of all God's people. They may feel themselves the helpless pawns of forces out of their control. Perhaps people even have what appear to be understandable motives for what they do wrong. But that does not lessen the responsibility of God's people to do right. Perhaps Potiphar unfairly pushed his wife out of her defining role in life. But that did not give Joseph any excuse to commit adultery with her. No matter how overwhelming the pressures against us may appear, we still have control over how we react.

Egypt was rather casual about sexual relationships except for adultery with another man's wife. Adultery shamed the husband of the adulterous woman. Yet Joseph did not defend his refusal to commit adultery with her on the grounds that it would dishonor Potiphar. Rather he saw it as dishonoring God. "How then could I do this great wickedness, and sin against God?" (Gen. 39:9). No matter how ethically difficult or complex a situation

God's people might find themselves in, they will always evaluate what they do by whether it will honor God.

Providence Wears a Human Face

Biblical chronology suggests that Joseph may have lived during the Hyksos period of Egyptian history (1750-1550 B.C.), when Asiatics rather than native Egyptians ruled the country.[20] The fact that the king or pharaoh and Joseph shared similar ethnic backgrounds may have encouraged him to trust in the Hebrew slave. As God worked out events for the future survival of Joseph and his family He did what He has constantly done in human history—He used human beings and human circumstances to accomplish His purposes. Because of the human mask God so often wears, His people, as in the case of Joseph himself, usually do not see God's guidance and providence until He has completed His plans. An observer in Pharaoh's court may have concluded that the king favored Joseph because of their common cultural ties—fellow Asiatics in a foreign land. But the king did not have to appoint Joseph second-in-command or even listen to his interpretation of the dreams. The Holy Spirit generally works through the familiar things of life. Both in great events and in the lives of believers, providence labors with the tools of the ordinary and the common. Only later will God open the eyes of faith so that people can see the marvelous things He has done.

The members of Pharaoh's court would have understood much of what happened. People in their world believed that the gods communicated to human beings through dreams. If it was a really important message to a ruler, the gods might emphasize that fact by sending a double dream.[21] The only thing unusual about this present experience was that the king needed help in interpreting the dream.[22] Since the Egyptian king was considered a god himself, he normally understood the divine messages. The Hebrew word that Genesis uses to describe the specialists Pharaoh sent for comes from a technical Egyptian term that some scholars believe refers to dream interpreters. A second-century B.C. inscription applies it to the court official Imhotep as he advises a pharaoh about an impending seven-year famine.[23]

Even Pharaoh's dreams employed familiar imagery. Cattle and stalks of grain were a part of everyday life. The cow was also the visible form of one of Egypt's major deities, the goddess Hathor. Famines frequently struck the ancient world, even in Egypt with its normally reliable source of water for irrigation, the river Nile. While the annual flooding of the Nile valley made Egypt more fertile and secure than most of the Middle East, too little or too much water could trigger a famine. People barely survived from one harvest to another, and anything that destroyed or reduced a crop's yield could plunge a whole society into disaster. Although they usually portrayed only idealistic scenes, Egyptian artists occasionally acknowledged the precariousness of life by depicting emaciated famine victims on the walls of tombs and public buildings. The Egyptian *Visions of Neferti,* dating to the reign of Amenemhet I (1991-1962 B.C.), describes a vision foretelling such a famine.[24] The famine that struck the ancient Near East in Joseph's time was not out of the ordinary. As Derek Kidner observes, Joseph does not describe the approaching famine as a judgment against Egypt or call for repentance. Rather it was "one of life's irregularities"[25] that God chose to employ for His own purposes. God daily works through the humdrum of each of our lives. We need to let Him open our eyes to see His providence in the ordinary things of life. If we do not learn to recognize God in the world of the ordinary, we will fail to see Him even in the miraculous.

Healing a Sick Family

As we have already seen, Jacob's family was an extremely dysfunctional one. God could not build a nation from a family that was destroying itself. He had to restore its many broken relationships. But to be healed we must first recognize that we have a disease. The brothers had to acknowledge their guilt before they could see any need for forgiveness. They had to accept responsibility for what they had done both to Joseph and to their father. Yes, both the younger dreamer-brother as well as Jacob had been flawed, but the brothers still had freely chosen how they would react to them.

The brothers came to Egypt to find food to survive the widespread famine. As they traveled back and forth between the land of the Nile and Canaan the Holy Spirit worked on their hearts to see and to accept the reality of what they had done to the brother whom they now believed to be long dead. When they appeared before him, Joseph tested them. Were they the same men who had almost killed him, then sold him into slavery? When he labeled them spies (Gen. 42:9-12) (the people of the surrounding nations were always trying to infiltrate the fertile Nile delta), they replied that they were honest men, 10 members of a family of 12 sons (verse 13). Why would they mention such a detail? Do we hear in their words the whispering of the Holy Spirit? Although we may come to feel and recognize our guilt, as fallen human beings we cannot accept responsibility for our sinful actions and thoughts without God's help. Only He can transform us, just as He enabled the brothers to admit to each other, "Alas, we are paying the penalty for what we did to our brother" (verse 21). They finally felt Joseph's "anguish when he pleaded with us."

As Joseph listened to them struggle to make sense of the frightening situations he plunged them into, he must have wanted to believe what he witnessed. But he had been hurt deeply. He too needed healing. God had to remove the pain of betrayal and abandonment in Joseph's heart. The brothers now sensed their need for forgiveness, and Joseph needed to give such forgiveness. Forgiveness was the key to all their healing. But forgiveness may take time to both receive and give. Joseph spent much time making sure that his brothers had changed. And it was also just as hard for them to accept. Even after their father died the brothers still wondered if Joseph had really forgiven them (Gen. 50:15-21).

The story of Joseph begins with a broken and estranged family. He was an immature young man with a sense of destiny but far from ready to fulfill it. The other brothers were violent and deceitful, true sons of their father, Jacob. Angry and frustrated by what

Jacob had done to them, they gave in to their hatred and avenged themselves on their father through the son he loved too much and too unwisely. But God was using both the ordinary and the extraordinary to transform them. Genesis 50:17, 18 tells us that the Spirit healed them to the point that they could weep together.

What had seemed at first only cruel and meaningless events had become in the hand of God a way to mature Joseph into a powerful leader who saved not only his family but also the whole nation of Egypt. That does not mean that God intended the brothers to abuse Joseph and sell him into slavery. The Lord sets the goal; then He may let human beings choose the means, whether for good or bad. But even if they opt for evil, He can bring good out of it (verse 20).

What the Lord did in Jacob's family He longs to do for all His children. We all need healing before we can live as a family for eternity.

---

[1] See Angel Manuel Rodríguez, *Esther: A Theological Approach* (Berrien Springs, Mich.: Andrews University Press, 1995), pp. 23, 39-41.

[2] Besides having the only other occurrence for the term used for Joseph's robe in Genesis 37:3, it follows the structure of the Joseph story in reverse order. Instead of triumph, as in the case of Joseph and the book of Esther, the story of Tamar leads to disaster and sorrow.

[3] See, for example, B. Malina and R. Rohrbaugh, *Synoptic Gospels*, in their comments on honor and shame. Although they focus on the New Testament period, the issue of honor and shame has existed throughout the history of the Mediterranean world, and still survives as a fundamental strand of the social fabric there even today.

[4] J. Walton and V. Matthews, *IVP Bible Background Commentary: Genesis-Deuteronomy*, p. 70. Many introductory books on the Old Testament have reproductions of the Beni-hasan tomb paintings.

[5] W. Brueggemann, *Genesis*, p. 300.

[6] *Harper Bible Commentary*, p. 112.

[7] *Ibid.*

[8] Walton and Matthews, p. 70.

[9] Notice that dreams come in pairs in the Joseph story.

[10] Derek Kidner considers "your mother" as referring to Leah, it being "unrealistic to make it imply that Rachel was still alive" (*Genesis*, p. 181).

[11] *Ibid.*

[12] J. Sanders, *The God Who Risks*, p. 75.

[13] Victor J. Matthews, *Manners and Customs of the Bible* (Peabody, Mass.: Hendrickson Publishers, 1988), pp. 9, 10.

[14] Walton and Matthews, p. 48.

[15] Leo G. Perdue, Joseph Blenkinsopp, John J. Collins, and Carol Meyers, *Families in Ancient Israel* (Louisville, Ky.: Westminster John Knox Press, 1997), p. 26.

[16] *Ibid.*

[17] Joyce Tyldesley, *Daughters of Isis: Women of Ancient Egypt* (London: Penguin, 1994), p. 82.

[18] Jacob wore Esau's clothing as well as animal skins on his arms to trick his father (Gen. 27). Tamar kept Jacob's signet seal that he wore on a cord (Gen. 38). And first Joseph's robe almost caused his death; then his tunic.

[19] Walton and Matthews, p. 74.

[20] See Jack Finegan, *Handbook of Biblical Chronology: Principles of Time Reckoning in the Ancient World and Problems of Chronology in the Bible*, rev. ed. (Peabody, Mass.: Hendrickson Publishers, 1998), pp. 207-224.

[21] Walton and Matthews, p. 75.

[22] *Ibid.*

[23] *Ibid.*

[24] *Ibid.*

[25] Kidner, p. 196.

CHAPTER 6

Siblings in Love and Hate

Throughout most of human history survival has depended on the support and protection of extended families. People had to work hard to wring a living from the land, and since they did not have machinery or other labor-saving devices, they needed large families to work the land or staff their home industries. Unlike the modern Western family, a child working on the family farm or around the home produced more than the child consumed.

Ancient families originated most of their food and clothing. They grew or made almost everything they needed, and children could help in that. Parents did not have to pay for expensive education. The extended family taught what boys and girls had to know. Toys and consumer goods oriented toward children did not take big bites out of a family's budget. The children started working as soon as they were able, and did not have much time to play. Each child was an economic asset, not a liability. The more children, the more financially secure the family would be.

The high child mortality rate of the ancient world put additional pressure on parents to have large families. Scripture does not deal directly with the high death rate of children, though we can detect hints of it in the constant longing of biblical women to be mothers. But archaeological and other evidence indicates the continual threats to survival that families faced. When Israel first settled in Canaan after the Exodus, women would have had nearly two pregnancies for every child that survived to the age of 5 (compared to a survival rate in the nineteenth century of five or six out of seven or eight live births).[1] The survival rate would have improved only slowly through the centuries. The safest bet would always be to have as many children as possible.

Biblical adults did not live in so-called nuclear families. When boys married they brought their wives home with them to live under the authority of the son's father. Girls would join their husbands' extended families. Iron Age I houses (the time of the conquest of Canaan and the Judges) were built in clusters sharing common walls and courtyards.[2] The multigenerational extended families would work together in the fields, prepare meals together, and share all other tasks.[3]

But while large families were absolutely necessary for survival, they had their own problems. Land and other resources were limited. As an extended family grows, how is the family inheritance passed down to the next generation without subdividing it into smaller and smaller parcels that eventually become too tiny to support anyone? Wills preserved in the dry sands of Egypt record such minuscule inheritances as the right to sleeping space in one room of the family home. Land was the biggest problem. A farm might start out with four acres of arable land. If two sons survived to adulthood and the family divided the land equally between them, they would receive only two acres each. The fact that several generations dwelled together would slow the process, but after a number of generations the land would have been subdivided into plots too small to sustain anyone at all.

The ancient world sought to keep a family estate intact and economically viable either by passing the land down as a complete unit to the eldest surviving son or—in the case of biblical society—by giving the eldest son a double portion (Deut. 21:17). In the biblical world daughters did not inherit land unless they had no male relative (Num. 27:1-11). Their inheritance would consist of clothing, jewelry, and household items. Daughters always married outside the immediate family and did not take land with them. Younger sons would remain under the authority of the father and his successor, the oldest brother in the family, or under the monarch might enter military service.[4] The latter was a pattern that would continue for thousands of years in Western society as younger sons fought in foreign wars, went to sea on ships, or traveled as merchants. Many of the settlers of North and

South America and Australia and New Zealand were younger sons who could not expect to inherit anything significant from the family estate and had to seek their fortunes elsewhere. But in the biblical world most sons had no choice but to remain in the extended family with its constant tensions of people living in confined quarters, struggling to survive on too limited resources. It was impossible to move to another city and find work there as modern young people do.

The harsh life of biblical times with its short life spans meant that in most cases a person's parents were dead by the time he or she reached puberty. If the parents did survive into relative old age, that created another set of problems. Carol Meyers observed that as grown children of aging parents assumed the physical labor that the latter could no longer do, they naturally also wanted to be involved in family decision-making. Adult children chafe under such subordination and restriction, even in societies built around the extended family. They want to take charge of their own lives.[5] Genesis is full of examples of such intergenerational conflict. Brothers (such as Jacob and Esau) struggle for power and control of family resources, and family members make shifting alliances in the ongoing conflict. Joseph's brothers chafed under their father's rule and especially resented his favoritism toward the sons of Rachel. Siblings also jockey for power and honor.

Modern society has made such interfamily conflict even more complicated with the development of step—or blended—families. Divorce and remarriage produce complex and confusing relationships. Incest and abuse damages families for generations. And family specialists struggle to treat dysfunctional families. But such problems are not new as we see when we read the stories of David's family. Amnon deliberately shames his half-brother Absalom by raping Absalom's full sister (and his half-sister) Tamar (2 Sam. 13). Absalom avenges Tamar by killing Amnon, then has to flee, severing his relationship with his father, David. The rivalry between the various half-siblings not only fracture David's family but undercut the credibility and authority of the monarchy.

Although modern individuals, especially in the Western world, live in different circumstances, there is still much we can learn from biblical siblings. Jacob's family is a classic illustration of the problems that can tear any family apart. Sibling rivalry appears throughout Scripture, beginning in the book of Genesis. We will also look at one of Christ's parables based on family relationships.

My Brother's Keeper?

Family problems appear immediately in human history, in the story of Cain and Abel. Biblical students often focus on the contrasting ways the two brothers worshiped God. Usually we regard Abel as an example of someone recognizing his or her need for a Saviour, and Cain as approaching religion through human works and efforts; that Abel put his dependence on God and Cain on self. But the difference between them is greater than that.

The Hebrew word for the two sacrifices is closely associated with the grain offering of Leviticus 2 and designates the brothers' offerings as "gifts." They apparently both brought them to express gratitude to God.[6] But Cain had no real gratitude in his heart. Genesis 4:4, 5 declares that "the Lord had regard for Abel and his offering, but for Cain and his offering he had no regard." The offerings reflect the giver. Thus the real problem was not with Cain's offering but with Cain himself. The biblical account does not explicitly tell us what was wrong with Cain, but instead lets us watch him in action and from his resulting behavior figure out his problem ourselves. Cain murdered his brother. Murder is the taking of life, something that belongs only to God. Following the footsteps of his parents, Cain wanted to be like God.[7] But would-be gods are self-centered. Unlike the true God, they do not care for others. And this was Cain's most fundamental problem. Derek Kidner sees him as arrogant. His whole life denied the meaning of his sacrifice.[8] The essence of biblical sacrifice is an acknowledgment of God, His authority, and His role and nature.

We observe Cain's self-centeredness and arrogance in the

answer he gave when God asked him, "Where is your brother Abel?" (Gen. 4:9). Cain replied, "I do not know; am I my brother's keeper?" (verse 9). The first murderer was indeed not his brother's keeper, though he should have been. Instead of accepting his brother and finding in Abel's relationship with God a model for both the human-human and divine-human relationships, Cain let his anger and rivalry grow into a raging beast that ruled his life. Countless siblings have followed Cain's example ever since.

God created human beings to care for each other. But sin always drives wedges between people. Those wedges or barriers can be jealousy, hate, blame, and an infinite list of other problems. When God asked Adam and Eve if they had eaten from the forbidden tree, they immediately began blaming both God and each other for what had happened. Adam shifted fault to "the woman whom *you* gave to be with me" (Gen. 3:12). She put responsibility on the serpent (verse 13) and, by implication, God also, since He had made the creature (verse 1). Sin denies responsibility for both personal behavior and the need for relationships with others. It also comes between us and God.

The barrier sin creates reached its most dramatic moment when Jesus became sin for us on the cross. He cried out in agony, "My God, my God, why have you forsaken me?" (Matt. 27:46). Sin made Jesus feel cast off from the Father even though the Father was right beside Him. Matthew reports that darkness covered the land (verse 45) and the earth shook (verse 51). Scripture uses darkness and earthquake as a symbol of God's presence, as we notice in Genesis 15:12; Exodus 19:16 and 18; and Psalm 104:32 (cf. Ps. 68:7, 8). But Jesus could not see a theophany—only His isolation. When Christ accepted our sin at Calvary it severed the intimate relationship and community of the Godhead.

Cain was not his brother's keeper. He thought he needed no one. Even his relationship with God was superficial at best. But when God told him that his punishment was to be a wanderer, he suddenly realized the necessity of community. He both feared other human beings (since he would no longer be in community with them) and struggled with the horror of being "hidden from your [God's] face" (Gen. 4:13, 14). The first son had a faint taste of what the only-begotten Son would someday have to experience to redeem humanity. Although Cain had been alienated from humanity and God for much of his life, he had not realized it until then. But even after he fled his family, he did not change, as we observe in verses 23 and 24. Having left "the presence of the Lord" (verse 16) in more ways than one, he never did learn what it meant to be his brother's keeper.

War in the Womb

Apart from the stories of David's sons, the narrative of Jacob and Esau offer the classic example of struggle between brothers for dominance within a family. The symbol of that struggle was the birthright. Modern commentators focus on what they see as the religious dimensions of the birthright, limiting the conflict to who would be the ancestor of the Messiah. But the issues were broader than that and would extend to succeeding generations. It would continue to tear apart Jacob's family simply because of what kind of person he was.

Scripture took the struggle between the twins so seriously that it portrays the conflict as beginning in the womb (Gen. 25:22). Although Esau was born first, Jacob symbolically displayed his lifelong character by gripping Esau's heel (verse 26). God had already told their mother, Rebekah, that the elder son would serve the younger (verse 23). For the rest of his life Jacob would be trying to fulfill that prophecy himself, always running ahead of God and making it difficult for the Lord to bring it to pass in His own way.

Bible readers often regard Esau as the evil brother and Jacob as the good one. Yet the biblical depiction is much more complex and depicts the good and bad of both. Walter Brueggemann notes that in Scripture this older brother "is handled carefully and respectfully all through this narrative." [9] The biblical author has not a single harsh word about Esau, depicting his anger toward Jacob (Gen. 27:34-41) "uncritically and not without justification."[10] The nearest Genesis comes to criticizing Esau is Genesis 26:34, 35, but the brother seeks to make amends in Genesis 28:6-9. Brueggemann here regards Scripture as complimenting Esau.[11] Above all, unlike his brother, Esau is never devious or deceptive.

Esau did treat the birthright due him as the firstborn too lightly. He traded it to his brother for a bowl of lentil stew (Gen. 25:29-34). But to Jacob it became an all-consuming passion. Later he willingly went along with his mother's scheme to deceive his father to obtain his father's blessing. Jacob had learned well from his parents the ability to deceive. Rebekah taught him how to trick his nearly blind father (Gen. 27:5-17). But even Isaac had a devious streak, as we observe in his encounter with King Abimelech (Gen. 26:6-16). And Isaac was only imitating his own father, Abraham (Gen. 12:10-20).

When Jacob fled to Paddan-aram to save his life (Gen. 28) he soon met his match in deceitfulness in his uncle Laban (Gen. 29). Jacob's life became an unending struggle with that equally cunning trickster. Deceitfulness soon infected his new family. Rachel tricked her father (Gen. 31:19-35), and both she and Leah manipulated Jacob himself (Gen. 30:14-17). But Jacob was still determined to fulfill God's prophecy to his mother in his own way.

God had to work hard and long to bring Jacob to a point at which he would let Him lead. When the patriarch thought he had prospered through his own efforts, increasing his flocks faster than Laban's despite the handicaps his uncle imposed on him, the Lord had to send a dream to set Jacob straight. In it God revealed that Jacob's success with his flocks was not his own doing, but God's (Gen. 31:10-12). Finally, when Jacob and his family fled Laban back to Canaan, God had to literally wrestle Jacob into submission (Gen. 32:22-32).

Esau had every reason to seek revenge against Jacob when he learned of his brother's return. Naturally, Jacob was afraid of meeting him. He divided his household into two sections for protection and sent gifts of animals ahead of him (Gen. 32). When the two brothers encountered each other, Jacob bowed seven times to Esau, perhaps signifying that he now considered himself a vassal to his brother (Gen. 33:3).[12] Jacob referred to Esau as "my lord" (verses 8, 14), continuing the theme of submission. The brother who had stolen the primacy of the birthright acknowledged the authority of the one he had seized it from. But Esau ran to embrace him, and they wept together (verse 4). He called Jacob "my brother" (verse 9).

Esau seems more reconciled to Jacob than Jacob does to his twin. The older brother accepts Jacob's gift, thus sealing that reconciliation.[13] It is a return of the stolen birthright and blessing. When Esau offers to accompany Jacob along his journey, the brother politely declines (verses 12, 13). After urging Esau to go on ahead because his household and flocks will not be able to keep up with the older brother, Jacob promises to "come to my lord in Seir" (verse 14), Esau's home. But Jacob then immediately heads north to Succoth (verse 17). The biblical account never does mention him going to Seir. Did he revert to his old trickster mentality? Or was he just afraid of Esau, unable to trust him because he was untrustworthy himself? Jacob also rejects Esau's offer of some of his retainers (verse 15). Clearly he does not fully trust Esau even though his brother makes no hostile moves.

The Bible mentions one final encounter between the brothers—at their father's death (Gen. 35:29). After burying Isaac, the brothers divide their households and flocks peacefully and settle some distance from each other in echo of the separation of Abraham and Lot (Gen. 36:6-9). No stigma falls on Esau.[14] Genesis gives a lengthy genealogy of Esau, showing his importance. As Abraham's two sons founded two nations (Gen. 21:13), so Isaac's sons would each found a nation.

"The free choice of Jacob by Yahweh (25:23) is sure and unchallenged in the narrative. But Esau is there, very much there."[15] Just because God elects Jacob does not mean He rejects Esau. When God changed Abram's name to Abraham, He told the patriarch that He would make "nations" of him (Gen. 17:6). Ishmael founded one nation and now Esau another. What could

God have accomplished if the two brothers—especially Jacob—had chosen a different way of relating to each other?

Who Claims to Speak for God?

One of the greatest temptations to religious people is the desire to become God's exclusive channel to humanity. They want Him to speak only through them. In Numbers 12:1, 2 Miriam and Aaron criticize their brother, Moses, because he has married a Cushite woman, but that is only a smoke screen for the real issue. It appears in two questions they raise: "Has the Lord spoken only through Moses? Has he not spoken through us also?" (verse 2). They do have a point. Exodus 15:20 describes Miriam as a prophet. And just previous to the incident in Numbers 12 the Holy Spirit spoke through 70 elders and then two men named Eldad and Medad (Num. 11:24-26). When Joshua tried to stop the latter (verse 28), Moses replied, "Are you jealous for my sake? Would that all the Lord's people were prophets, and that the Lord would put his spirit on them!" (verse 29).

But Miriam and Aaron are not trying to increase the number of God's spokespersons—they want to be in charge of the divine channels. Moses is their younger brother. Why should he have greater authority than they? God should be leading His people through them—not through the brother they had helped to raise. Even God's most devoted servants can succumb to the desire for power and position. Miriam and Aaron added to that temptation sibling rivalry.

The struggle for religious power was bad enough, but to do it within the family of Israel's leader made it far worse. Moses already had had to deal with a number of cases of rebellion, mostly among the common people or nonleaders. Now insurrection infiltrated his own family. Moses' reputation and authority were at stake. If the people turned against him, it could shatter them as a nation and destroy everything that the Exodus had accomplished. God could not let Miriam and Aaron challenge their brother. He had to take drastic steps to deal with it.

The Hebrews had just come from centuries of life in Egypt.

The Egyptian gods consisted of sets of brothers and sisters who often struggled for power, sometimes resorting to deceit and even murder to get their way. In chapter 1 we mentioned the brothers Horus and Seth, who fought each other for rulership of the gods, often playing one divine faction against another. The Lord of Israel could not let such a concept infect His people. Nor could He permit Miriam and Moses to model a pattern of family strife. Also, a number of times during the 40 years of wandering God had to demonstrate that He alone chose His representatives. They did not appoint themselves.

Too Busy Doing Good

Popular devotional thought assumes that the difference between the sisters Mary and Martha was that Mary was spiritual and Martha was too concerned about practical matters. But the issue runs deeper than that.

Martha had invited Jesus into her home. She was His host. Hospitality was a most sacred aspect of biblical culture, touching as it did one of the most vital relationships in human society. In a world without hotels, restaurants, and highway patrols, people could survive only as they helped each other along the way. "Most of the ancient world regarded hospitality as a fundamental moral practice. It was necessary to human well-being and essential to the protection of vulnerable strangers. Hospitality assured strangers at least a minimum of provision, protection, and connection with the larger community. It also sustained the normal network of relationships on which a community depended, enriching moral and social bonds among family, friends and neighbors." [16]

The Bible often depicts God's people acting as good hosts (e.g., Abraham, Gen. 18:6-8). It condemned those who did not behave as good hosts (Gen. 19:1-11; Judges 19:15, 18). Hospitality or inhospitality revealed the inherent good or evil of a person or community. [17] Jesus used imagery of hosts in His parables (Luke 11:5-8; 14:12-14). Psalm 23 is as much about being a good host as it is being about a good shepherd. Even today Middle Eastern culture highly values hospitality.

In light of the mandatory role and responsibility of being a host in the biblical world, Martha was fulfilling a sacred duty when she welcomed Jesus into her home (Luke 10:38). But even sacred things may need to be put aside if they come between us and our Saviour. She discovered this fact when she complained about her sister, Mary, who sat at Jesus' feet listening to His teaching. In Martha's culture women worked behind the scenes and men alone discussed religious, philosophical, and other issues. Not only was Mary not helping her sister; she was violating social code by acting like a male! She was shaming her family by sitting in public in the presence of men.[18] Within the worldview of her time Martha's complaint was quite legitimate. She was doing what a reputable woman should, and Mary was being a public spectacle. Thus in New Testament times nobody would have questioned her right to ask Jesus to make Mary fulfill her sacred responsibility and help her sister with the duties of a good host (Luke 10:40).

Jesus ignores the social rules of His world, however. He tells Martha that she has let herself get too distracted. "There is need of only one thing," He explains to her.[19] "Mary has chosen the better part, which will not be taken away from her" (verse 42). One scholar, after examining some of the Greek terminology used of Martha, has suggested that since the same words also refer to church leaders in the New Testament, Martha may symbolize church leaders who become so busy working for Jesus that they forget to take the time to have a close relationship with Him. Leon Morris notes that Luke places the incident right after the parable of the good Samaritan so that readers would not interpret it as teaching that salvation is by works.[20]

Even good things can come between us and God. Because Jesus loved Martha so much, He wanted that nothing should diminish that relationship. In John 11 when Jesus arrives at her home after the death of Lazarus, Mary remains at home while Martha rushes out to meet Jesus (verse 20), reversing the previous roles of the two sisters. After telling Him that her brother wouldn't have died if He had been there (verse 21), Martha adds, "But even now I know that God will give you whatever you ask of him" (verse 22). Could this be an indication of a deepening relationship with Jesus as she now seeks "the better part" (Luke 10:42)?

The Elder Brother

The final example of sibling relations that we will look at appears in a parable but accurately reflects life.

As we have already noted, in the biblical world the main source of wealth was land. When the younger son in Luke's parable asked his father for his share of the inheritance, the only way the father could give it to him was to sell some of the family land, land that would have gone to the older brother. Now with less land, the family might not be able to grow enough to feed itself and earn cash at the market to pay taxes and other expenses. What the father did was comparable to cashing in the family retirement account to pay for current expenses. The funds would be gone when needed later.

Normally sons received their inheritance only when the father died. The younger son, by demanding his inheritance early, was in effect symbolically calling for the death of his father. As for the older brother, in addition to threatening his own inheritance, the younger brother's demand would have offended him because it showed a lack of respect for the father.

When the father sold some of the family property to raise cash to give to the younger son, it would have provoked hostility also among the local villagers. They would not want their sons getting the same idea, and would have felt resentment toward the father and the rest of the family for giving in to the demand. The older son would daily encounter the strong, if not always verbalized, feelings of their neighbors.[21] It was tension created by the outrageous behavior of his younger brother.

Then the prodigal has the audacity to return home. And what does the father do? He disgraces himself and humiliates the older brother by racing to meet the younger son (Luke 15:20). In biblical culture this was an undignified act.[22] After excitedly kissing him (in the manner of Middle Eastern culture), the father puts a ceremonial robe over the youth's dirty rags and sandals on his feet, then slips a signet ring on the son's finger and calls for a celebration (verses 20-23). The clothing, shoes, and ring indicate that the younger son had been accepted back as a full member of the family.[23]

As the older son comes from his work in the fields he hears the sounds of celebration. Since biblical culture had no way of preserving meat, the fattened calf had to be eaten immediately, and undoubtedly the father had invited a large number of guests, if not the whole village, to consume it.[24] Probably having an idea of what was going on, the older brother does not join the party but summons a servant to find out if his worst fears are true (verse 26). When the servant confirms the nature of the celebration, the older brother angrily refuses to go inside (verse 28). Not to be part of the party and act his role as host with the father insults not only his brother but the entire village. The father again humiliates himself when he goes outside to plead with the older son (verse 28).[25] The older brother insults his father again by refusing to use any title of respect.[26] Then he calls his brother "this son of yours" (verse 30) to show that he has not accepted the prodigal back into the family.

While the older brother had many reasons to resent what the younger one did, his behavior did not show love. But perhaps we can see the most important lesson that Jesus wanted us to learn when we ask ourselves who the two brothers would have depicted in the minds of His hearers. The older brother represented God's people, and the younger the Gentiles who have yet to come to Him. Today we might also compare the older brother to those who have long and faithfully served God, and the younger to those who have rebelled against God or even abandoned Him, only to return in repentance. Sometimes those of us who have faithfully worked for God and carefully obeyed His commandments may feel uncomfortable with the idea that God so easily forgives and accepts those who have boldly sinned and turned their backs on Him. But did the father love the older brother less even though he welcomed the younger brother back with a feast?

The older brother would have been willing to accept his brother back to penitence but not to celebration. What the father did seemed too much like condoning the prodigal's sin.[27] But the Father loves all His children, and older brothers miss much when they do not share His joy.

---

[1] L. Perdue, J. Blenkinsopp, J. Collins, and C. Meyers, *Families in Ancient Israel*, p. 28.

[2] *Ibid.*, p. 16.

[3] Since several generations lived together in a home at any one time, Exodus 20:5 speaks of God punishing children of the third and fourth generations. The constant proximity would generally make everyone involved in what any individual person did.

[4] *Ibid.*, p. 35.

[5] *Ibid.*

[6] J. Walton and V. Matthews, *IVP Bible Background Commentary: Genesis-Deuteronomy*, p. 22.

[7] *Harper's Bible Commentary*, p. 89.

[8] D. Kidner, *Genesis*, p. 75.

[9] W. Brueggemann, *Genesis*, p. 285.

[10] *Ibid.*

[11] *Ibid.*

[12] Fifteenth-century B.C. Egyptian texts from El Armana tell of vassals bowing seven times to the pharaoh (Walton and Matthews, p. 66).

[13] Kidner, p. 171.

[14] Brueggemann, *Genesis*, p. 285.

[15] *Ibid.*, p. 286.

[16] C. Pohl, *Making Room*, p. 17. Pohl's book not only examines the biblical background and teaching on hospitality, but also traces its practice within Christianity to the present day.

[17] *Ibid.*, p. 26.

[18] B. Malina and R. Rohrbaugh, *Synoptic Gospels*, p. 348.

[19] Some commentators have seen Jesus as declaring that she had prepared too elaborate a meal, that one dish would have been sufficient (*Harper's Bible Commentary*, p. 1029). Leon Morris rejects such an interpretation as being contrary to the language of the passage (Leon Morris, *Luke: An Introduction and Commentary*, rev. ed. [Leicester, Eng.: InterVarsity Press, 1988], p. 210).

[20] *Ibid.*, p. 209.

[21] Malina and Rohrbaugh, *Synoptic Gospels*, p. 371.

[22] J. Sanders, *The God Who Risks*, p. 109.

[23] Malina and Rohrbaugh, *Synoptic Gospels*, p. 372.

[24] *Ibid.*

[25] Sanders, pp. 109, 110.

[26] *Ibid.*, p. 110.

[27] *Harper's Bible Commentary*, p. 1034.

CHAPTER 7

Suffer the Children

Life was hard in the ancient world, especially for children. Graves and other archaeological data indicate an infant mortality rate of up to 30 percent. Thirty percent of those born alive were dead from accident, disease, or malnutrition by age 6, and 60 percent perished by age 16. Seventy percent lost one or both parents before reaching puberty.[1] When Jesus blessed the children that their mothers brought to Him (Matt. 19:13-15), both He and they knew that a high percentage of the young people would be dead before the next year rolled around.[2]

Unlike in the modern world, childhood was a fleeting period of life. Children began to help around the home almost as soon as they could walk. As early as 5 or 6, both boys and girls would gather fuel, care for even younger children, water and pick vegetables, and assist in cooking and other food preparation. Young children usually assisted women. By 7 or 8, children might work up to four hours a day. When they reached 13, they would be doing adult tasks for as long as nine hours a day, usually with adults of the same sex.[3]

Girls quickly learned cooking, spinning wool and flax, and other household duties. Both boys and girls helped in the fields and with the flocks. Boys lived in the world of women until about 7 or 8, then had an abrupt and traumatic transition to the stern world of men, though they did receive more pampering than girls did. Mothers breast-fed male children twice as long as girls. Once boys entered the world of men they had to shed all feminine traits and display their masculinity through displays of courage and sexual aggression.[4]

Adulthood came extremely early. Girls would remain in the

home until betrothed and married, usually in their early teens. Biblical society considered a boy as an adult by the time he turned 13, though he married a little later than his sisters. Life was short, and young people had to raise a family as soon as possible. Only a handful of children—almost all of them from wealthier homes— had any kind of formal education. The home was the school, with the women as the first teachers, then the extended family. After the boys joined the world of men, they were apprenticed to their fathers, uncles, and grandfathers to learn the skills and specialized knowledge they would need to farm the rugged hills of Palestine.[5] Fathers had relatively little involvement in raising young children. Most Bible readers assume, for example, that Hosea 11:3 is a father speaking, yet then—as even now—mothers teach infants to walk.

The Eternal Challenge of Being a Parent

Parenting has always been a challenge. Throughout history society has failed or succeeded for a variety of complex reasons. We will look at examples of both.

The first example involves the sons of the priest Eli, Hophni and Phinehas. According to 1 Samuel 2:12-17 they were "scoundrels," seizing extra food from the offerings. The sacrifices provided a major source of priestly income, but the sons of Eli abused the privilege, casting disrespect on the priesthood and the sacrificial system. The fact that they would grab the meat while it was still boiling shows their great greed. When they divided the fat of the offering (verse 16) the worshipers who had brought the sacrifices protested that the fat belonged to God Himself, indicating that the common people were better protectors of the divine law than the young priests.[6]

They also forced themselves sexually on the women who served at the sanctuary at Shiloh (verse 22). The biblical author regards the women as part of the sanctuary's official personnel.[7] Hophni and Phinehas abused not only the people coming to the sanctuary, but its staff as well.[8] Scripture calls them, as it does the boy Samuel, *na'ar* ("young men"),[9] suggesting that they were by today's standards still extremely young.

Eli condemns their behavior, demanding, "Why do you do such things?" (verse 23). He tells them that knowledge of their behavior has spread throughout both the Shiloh community and elsewhere (verse 24). Many modern readers interpret Eli's protests as weak, but his words are actually quite blunt. "If one person sins against another, someone can intercede for the sinner with the Lord; but if someone sins against the Lord, who can make intercession?" (verse 25). How much clearer could he be? Their father argues that they have challenged God in such a way that "his goodwill can no longer be invoked." [10] The sons refuse to listen to him. Eli's sons could not claim ignorance as an excuse, "and their high-handed arrogance cried out for a fall (cf. vv. 2, 9, 10a)." [11] Although the problem is with his sons, Eli will pay the price by losing everything, following the biblical tradition that one generation can share responsibility for what another one does (Ex. 20:5; Jer. 32:18). [12] The priesthood will pass to another family line (verses 27-36).

The biblical account contrasts Eli's sons with the young Samuel. As Samuel matures spiritually, they degenerate. [13] The author depicts Samuel as a priest who will ultimately replace Eli. [14] But our concern here is with the sons' rejection of God and their abuse of their priestly duties. Scripture does not explain why they turned out as they did. Most modern readers assume that the responsibility rests solely on Eli's shoulders. The priest may have ignored and failed to discipline them. But he does not bear all the blame. The entire community of Shiloh must also share it. And their failure has a powerful lesson for the Christian community today.

Not until recently did parents raise children solely by themselves. The so-called nuclear family is a late phenomenon, developing in the Western world only after the rise of the Industrial Revolution. Until the appearance of factories, fathers worked at or near the home with the rest of the extended family. Aunts and uncles, grandparents, and even neighbors helped raise children. The people of the community would teach the neighborhood children life skills and even discipline them if they saw the youngsters behaving in ways that they knew their parents would not approve. The whole village played a vital role in a child's upbringing.

Everyone shared the responsibility of shaping young lives. Today—at least in the Western world—children do not usually live near relatives, and neighbors have little or no interest in the young people around them as long as the youngsters are not getting into trouble.

Eli was not the only one who failed his sons; so did the rest of the community living around the sanctuary. People gossiped about the sons (verse 23), but they apparently did little about the situation. They let the sons get away with their unforgivable behavior. While Hophni and Phinehas had to accept ultimate responsibility for their actions, the poor upbringing they received allowed them to slide more easily into evil. Fortunately the community of Shiloh did better with Samuel. The female sanctuary servants as well as the other women of the community acted as surrogate mothers for the child. They built upon what Hannah had already accomplished during those vital first years of the boy's life. His parents also kept contact with Samuel, visiting him at the time of the yearly sacrifice (1 Sam. 2:19).

The role a whole community has in raising a child is a lesson God's people need to remember today. All the adults in a congregation have a vital part to play in helping a church's children. They should serve as role models and mentors. This is especially important when so many single parents are trying to bring up children by themselves. Even children with two parents may have only one of them in the church. All members of a congregation must band together to support the children in their midst.

Only a Boy Named David

Readers have interpreted individuals in a number of biblical stories as young children when they really were not. As pointed out earlier, childhood was a fleeting experience in the ancient world. People had to accept adult responsibilities at ages we would regard as still part of childhood. The people of the time, however, considered them as fully adults. The familiar story of

David and his encounter with Goliath is one example.

The men of ancient armies had to supply their own food and often their own weapons and other equipment. Soldiers either brought their food with them from home or scavenged for it as they traveled across the country. Jesse's three oldest sons had joined Saul's army, and their father was responsible for supporting them. He sent David—whom he had kept home to tend the vital flocks—to the Israelite encampment at Elah with grain, bread, and cheese (1 Sam. 17:17, 18). Also, the father wanted to find out if the sons were still alive.[15] As David went to Saul's military base taking supplies to his older brothers, he carried a secret he could not share: he was to be the new king of God's people.

When the Israelites had clamored for a king like the surrounding nations (1 Sam. 8) they had especially wanted a strong ruler to lead them in resisting the invading Philistines. The Philistines, one of a number of peoples fleeing unsettled conditions in the Aegean Sea region, had migrated south until stopped by the Egyptians. Making a peace treaty with Pharaoh, they settled the coast of Palestine. Soon they began to push inland into the hill country where the Israelites lived. The Philistines were much more advanced militarily than the hastily assembled peasant armies of Israel.

God gave in to Israel's request. He directed Samuel to anoint Saul, son of Kish and a member of the tribe of Benjamin, as king. Saul seemed to have all the physical attributes that the people expected in a king. The long genealogy listed in 1 Samuel 9:1, 2 indicates that Saul belonged to an important family in the tribe, and in addition he had unusual stature and good looks. "He was outstandingly well endowed."[16] The young man was everything the people could have hoped for in a ruler. But the king eventually proved a disappointment as he drifted away from his relationship with God. The break between him and the Lord reached its climax during the incident at Gilgal.

Saul's army and the Philistine forces faced each other at Michmash (1 Sam. 13:5). The Israelite king did not want to engage the invaders until the prophet Samuel had first offered sacrifice. Such a sacrifice would have had "the political effect of evoking and underscoring the religious commitment so crucial to the 'war effort.'" [17] The king expected the prophet to arrive within seven days (verse 8). Unfortunately, the war had not been going well for Israel, and the Philistine military might so terrorized the peasant soldiers that they began to desert. Almost exclusively a volunteer force, they could not be expected to have the discipline of the more experienced Philistine army. Thus, Saul knew that if Samuel did not arrive soon he would have no army left.

In an act of desperation Saul decided to officiate at the burnt offering himself. But the king had no right to do so. He was imitating the pagan kings of the time. The Egyptian pharaoh and the Mesopotamian rulers might be the chief priests of their respective national religions, but not the king of Israel. Saul was "not authorized to offer sacrifice (cf. 9:13). He [was] authorized to act as judge and warrior, but not as priest. That crucial social role [had] been retained by Samuel for himself." [18] The king knew that he had no right to conduct sacrifices.

As soon as Saul finished the ritual, Samuel appeared and demanded, "What have you done?" (verse 11). Greatly upset with the king, the prophet told him that he had acted foolishly and broken God's commandment. If Saul had obeyed God, his kingdom would have lasted forever (verse 13). But now God would replace him with someone else, someone "after his [God's] own heart" (verse 14). Many commentators have had a hard time understanding Samuel's reaction. Brueggemann, for example, observes that Saul gave "an extended and reasoned explanation of his action in offering the sacrifice," that "Saul did not offer the sacrifice greedily, eagerly, aggressively, or to preempt the power of the old priesthood." [19] Hertzberg comments that "if anything is in the wrong here it is Samuel, and not Saul." [20] But as he points out, we have to examine this incident in light of Saul's whole life. [21]

Israel had wanted a king like the other nations, and that is what they got. In Egypt Pharaoh was believed to be a god who preserved order and prosperity in the land. He personally held chaos in check. Although Mesopotamia did not usually regard its kings as divine, it also saw its rulers as responsible for maintaining peace and prosperity. But God's people needed to remember always that their success depended on their obedience to the God of Israel, not to the power of their king. Saul had begun his rule with a strong sense of his ultimate powerlessness and his need for God (1 Sam. 9:21). He even hid when Israel chose him by lot (1 Sam. 10:20-22). But he soon became comfortable with kingship and began to think like other kings. He saw Israel's fate as dependent on what he did, not on God and His power.

As God watched Saul's transformation and deterioration, He realized that He had to choose another king. The Lord told Samuel, "I regret that I made Saul king, for he has turned back from following me, and has not carried out my commands" (1 Sam. 15:11). "The Lord was sorry that he had made Saul king over Israel" (verse 35). As a result God secretly sent Samuel to anoint someone else as Israel's ruler. He directed the prophet to the family of Jesse the Bethlehemite (1 Sam. 16:1). Jesse's oldest son immediately attracted Samuel (priority in biblical culture naturally went to the firstborn or oldest), but God told the prophet, "Do not look on his appearance or on the height of his stature, because I have rejected him; for the Lord does not see as mortals see; they look on the outward appearance, but the Lord looks on the heart" (verse 7). Physical appearance had impressed God's people once, but Saul had shrunk spiritually.

God next passed over the rest of the sons (verses 8-10), and finally Samuel had to ask if all the sons were present. David, the youngest, was out tending the sheep. The Lord told the prophet to anoint him.

The Right to Be All That You Can

Modern readers have so accepted the biblical principle that God judges a person by the heart (the ancient symbol of all that a person was) that they do not sense how startling the incident would have been to the people of the time. In the ancient world people almost always stayed in the social position they had been born in. Their family's socioeconomic standing and their gender and birth order assigned them a place and role in life in which they would remain until they died. Life was a hierarchy with a divinely ordained niche for everybody, and everyone should stay there no matter what their inherent abilities might be. The pattern was the same elsewhere in the ancient Near East.

In fact, it was so unusual, for example, for a commoner or person of lower social order to rise to a position of power that when it did happen such individuals and their supporters circulated special stories explaining how they had come to prominence, usually at the intervention of a divine being. Sargon the Great, the Semite king of Akkad who usurped the throne of the Sumerian king Ur-Zababa, claimed that his mother give birth to him in secret, then put him in a pitch-coated basket and floated him on the river. A water-drawer found him and raised him as a farmer. Other examples of Near Eastern rulers who used similar miraculous stories to legitimize their irregular backgrounds included Amenemhet I and Hatshepsut of Egypt and Hattusilis of Mesopotamia.[22]

In the Bible, birth order determined a son's place in life. Both custom and biblical law gave the firstborn special privileges (cf. Gen. 48:13, 14, 17, 18; Deut. 21:15-17; 2 Chron. 21:3). When Jesse brought his sons to Samuel, the prophet naturally assumed that Eliab, the firstborn (1 Sam. 17:13) would be God's choice. But God skipped over him and chose David, the youngest, instead.

At Saul's military camp David asked the soldiers what the king would give the individual who accepted Goliath's challenge "and takes away the reproach from Israel" (1 Sam. 17:26). Eliab immediately became angry at his youngest brother (verse 28). He accused David of abandoning the family flocks in the wilderness just so he could watch a battle. "What have I done?" David asked in frustration. "It was only a question" (verse 29).

Part of Eliab's reaction might have come from his feeling that the younger brother's comment about "reproach" was an implied criticism of Eliab and the other soldiers. Joyce Baldwin suggests that Eliab responded in anger because David "presumes to enter their military world, and implies that he may supersede them."[23] The younger son forgot his place in life and wanted to climb above it.

Saul had earlier offered whoever was willing to battle the Philistine champion[24] riches and his daughter. In addition, the king would "make his family free in Israel" (verse 25). Being married to the king's daughter would elevate her husband's social status and even give him a claim on the throne.[25] Baldwin comments that the last gift, which would exempt the victor's family from service to the king at court, was equivalent to being equal to the king himself.[26]

The idea of a youngest son trying to enter the royal family and make himself higher than his brothers irritated Eliab. The whole idea violated the social and religious rules he lived by and was an insult to him as the firstborn. Such a thought was in essence to turn the world upside down. David, as youngest son, should content himself with tending sheep and bringing supplies to his older brothers. That is what his position in life demanded of him.

Today we think nothing of a person seizing every opportunity and climbing his or her way up in the world through ability and determination. Nineteenth-century Americans liked to read stories about Horatio Alger-type characters who pulled themselves out of adversity and succeeded in life. Americans still like to believe that any citizen can become president of the United States. The public admires people who overcome disadvantages and accomplish great things. This willingness to allow people to advance themselves has spread throughout the Western world. Modern society feels that if people have abilities and gifts, they should use them. Social or economic status should hinder no one.

The Bible helped make such a world possible. The many stories in which God chose someone instead of the firstborn or ignored social and economic status helped break down the concept of a hierarchical world order. If God judged people by who they were on the inside, so should we. God selects by innate ability and—most important of all—by an individual's relationship and loyalty to Him. Israel had admired Saul because of his stature and looks. But its first king did not remain faithful to God. David protested Israel's cowardice before Goliath because it implied His people lacked faith in the "living God" (1 Sam. 17:26). They refused to glorify the God of Israel by showing their trust in Him.[27]

God had Samuel anoint David because of the youngest son's trust and relationship with Him. Despite all the terrible things that David did during his life, he never abandoned that loyalty. He was a man after God's heart.

When David defeated Goliath, he again demonstrated that physical stature is not what counts, but the inner relationship with God. Goliath might be awesome in a physical sense, but David was far greater spiritually. As for David being "only a little boy," the fact that Saul would consider him as a potential son-in-law indicates that he was an adult and of marriageable age in his culture.

Mauled by a Bear

Another incident that many Bible readers assume is about little children appears in 2 Kings 2:23, 24. The idea that a prophet would curse a group of boys just because they shouted at him, "Go away, baldhead" (verse 23) shocks modern readers. The implication that the prophetic curse led to she-bears waddling out of the woods to maul defenseless children compounds the horror. But to understand this story we must put it in its historical and cultural context.

First, the boys were not as young as we assume. Scripture uses the Hebrew word translated into English as "little children" or "small boys" in this passage for servants or individuals who were of marriageable age in biblical times, though we would consider them teenagers today.[28] The boys could not be extremely young children, because they would have been at home in the custody of their families and helping with the family work.

Elisha lived in a world that taught children to respect adults, especially religious leaders. Only during times of extreme social breakdown would young people have treated the prophet with such disrespect. Earlier we mentioned that by age 13 boys worked up to nine hours a day. The fact that these young people were wandering away from the fields and pastures where they would normally be working suggests a serious collapse of the biblical economy and social order. Young people in the ancient world did not have the free time that modern teenagers do.

Donald Wiseman suggests that since the incident took place near Bethel, the location of a major cultic site for the rival religious system of the northern kingdom of Israel, it may reflect hostility toward the true worship of Yahweh. The young people were echoing what they had heard among older adults. Verse 24 states that the two bears attacked 42 boys. That is a most unusually large number of young people to roam the countryside and get into trouble instead of working. They were bandits, perhaps comparable to a modern urban gang.

Elijah had just recently gone to heaven after passing his prophetic authority to Elisha (verses 1-14). If ignored, the boys' ridicule would have undercut Elisha's influence with the people. Whether they were telling him to "go up" in parody of Elijah's ascension or just to "go away" (NRSV), they were trying to destroy his prophetic role. Nothing can damage credibility and influence with others faster than ridicule and sarcasm. Elisha had to take drastic action to reverse the situation.

The fact that the bears attacked the boys showed the rest of the people how seriously God regarded the young mob's action. As the news spread about the incident, it instilled a sense of caution and perhaps even awe toward Elisha. It was something their culture could understand. The prophet was a man that people must take seriously. Today God might have His prophet respond in a different way toward disrespect of His servants. He would react in a manner that would suit the modern situation and culture.

Witness in a Foreign Land

A young person appears briefly in 2 Kings 5:2-4. Some commentators barely give her a glance. But she would have an international influence, and would be an agent to demonstrate the universality of the God of Abraham, Isaac, and Jacob.

Naaman, commander of the royal army in the bordering Syrian state of Aram, captured the girl, unnamed in the Bible, during a raid into the northern kingdom of Israel. The main source of slaves in the ancient world was warfare. The girl was Naaman's's booty, and he gave her to his wife as a servant.

The ancients believed that their gods accompanied their armies to battle. We see something similar to this idea whenever the Old Testament speaks of the God of Israel and Judah going to war for His people. But the people of the Near East also assumed that if they lost a battle it was because the god of the enemy defeated their deity. Naturally the Bible rejects such a concept, though sometimes we see the people of Israel struggling with the pagan belief. The Jews taken into exile wondered if they should now worship the gods of their captors or remain loyal to Yahweh.

Naaman would have assumed after he captured the servant girl that Rimmon, his national god, had defeated Yahweh. In the shock and discouragement of being taken to a distant land, the Israelite girl herself may have felt tempted to agree with him. But she clung to the God of Israel and Judah. And she worshiped in the old way, not the syncretistic religion mixing Yahwehism and pagan influences and rival cult centers that the rulers of the northern kingdom had introduced into her homeland of Israel.

Perhaps she had listened to the village elders discuss Elisha and his predecessor, Elijah. Some would have argued that the two prophets were troublemakers and disloyal to the state. They questioned their roles and mission. Others would have supported the campaign to reform the worship of the northern kingdom. The Israelite girl chose to follow Yahweh and His prophet Elisha.

When Naaman discovered that he had leprosy,[29] the girl remembered the miracles performed by God's prophet. Perhaps Elisha would cure her master's disease. "If only my lord were with the prophet who is in Samaria!" she exclaimed to Naaman's wife. "He would cure him of his leprosy" (verse 3). The girl radiated such conviction that the woman persuaded her husband to go to Elisha. Naaman in turn told his ruler about the prophet, and the king began the arrangements for Naaman to visit the Israelite healer, prophet of a foreign deity (verses 4, 5).

After his healing Naaman could have returned to the gods of Aram. It was not uncommon for the people of the ancient world to seek help from one god while remaining loyal to another. But instead he vowed to worship Yahweh (verse 17). His servant girl's conviction and the power demonstrated by the God of Israel confirmed that Yahweh was indeed the true all-powerful God of the universe.

It is interesting how the Old Testament often involves women when the God of Israel and Judah reveals His universal aspect. We see such non-Israelites as Hagar, Rahab, and Ruth responding to His power. Rahab and Ruth appear in Matthew's genealogy of Jesus. The women foreshadow His mission to the Gentile nations and the acceptance of the early Christian community of non-Jews.[30] Jesus sends His disciples to all nations with the good news of their inclusion in God's steadfast love.[31] Here in 2 Kings a girl leads a foreign official to acknowledge Yahweh. And Esther will later be involved in a series of events that will bring many non-Jews to her God (Esther 8:17).

The Child Kings

As we have noted, childhood in the biblical world was short, and it is sometimes difficult to know, when Scripture mentions a young person, whether people would have considered him or her a child or an adult. But the Old Testament records two individuals who were clearly children, even from the biblical perspective. They are two boys who became kings at an extremely young age. The high mortality rate and short life spans in the ancient world often caused royal heirs to find themselves on the throne while still children.

Jehoash[32] began to reign in Judah at 7 years of age (2 Kings 11:21), and Josiah at 8 years of age (2 Kings 22:1). Naturally a regent or some other adult would handle most of the practical details of rulership until the boy reached what the royal court considered sufficient maturity to assume direct rule. Scripture remembers Jehoash for his restoration of the Temple (2 Chron. 24). Later, though, Jehoash would strip that Temple to bribe the Syrian king Hazael not to attack Jerusalem (2 Kings 12:18). Second Chronicles describes him as faithful to God as long as his protector and mentor, the priest Jehoiada, lived. Jehoiada had arranged the palace coup that put Jehoash on the throne.

But Jehoash had a stronger relationship with the priest of God than he did with the God Jehoiada served. As has been too common in human governments, Jehoiada followed the advice of his counselors rather than making his own decisions. After Jehoiada's death Jehoash followed the lead of other court officials, people not as loyal to the God of Judah. He abandoned the God of his people and worshiped the deities of the surrounding nations.

The court officials probably urged the introduction of foreign worship as a way of making political allegiances with other nations. In the ancient world, government and national religion were for all practical purposes identical. Judah was a small kingdom, often warring with superpowers, and the court officials felt that it needed all the support it could get. Jehoiada's son Zechariah protested his policies. Jehoash had him assassinated (2 Chron. 24:21), only to die later at the hands of his own courtiers (verses 25, 26).

But Josiah remained faithful to God. He was not just the reflection of his advisors. Some scholars regard the book of Kings as depicting him as the greatest of all the kings of Judah (see 2 Kings 23:25).[33] Jehoash restored the Temple and eradicated pagan worship as long as the priest Jehoiada lived. A devout mentor guided his spiritual relationship. Unfortunately that relationship died with the priest. But Josiah had a personal relationship with the Lord. Like Jehoash, Josiah repaired the Temple. During its reconstruction the high priest found in it "the book of the law" (most probably the book of Deuteronomy) (2 Kings 22). Josiah also restored the observance of Passover and did everything possible to reform his nation. Huldah, as a prophet of God, told him that his efforts would ultimately fail, but that did not stop him from trying. He would follow the principles of his people's true faith regardless of the consequences—unlike Jehoash. The young kings chose very different paths through life.

---

[1] B. Malina and R. Rohrbaugh, *Synoptic Gospels*, p. 117.

[2] The mothers would have been seeking for Jesus to protect the children from the curse of the evil eye, the jealousy of others, the most feared menace in the Mediterranean world (ibid., pp. 122, 123).

[3] L. Perdue, J. Blenkinsopp, J. Collins, and C. Meyers, Families in Ancient Israel, p. 27.

[4] Malina and Rohrbaugh, Synoptic Gospels, p. 300.

[5] Perdue, Blenkinsopp, Collins, and Meyers, p. 30.

[6] Hans Wilhelm Hertzberg, I and II Samuel: A Commentary (Philadelphia: Westminster Press, 1964), p. 35.

[7] Scripture uses the same verb (ṣābā') of the women servants as it does of the Levites (e.g., Num. 4:23; 8:24) (J. Baldwin, 1 & 2 Samuel: An Introduction and Commentary, p. 60).

[8] Hertzberg, p. 36.

[9] Walter Brueggemann, First and Second Samuel, p. 22.

[10] Hertzberg, p. 36.

[11] Baldwin, p. 61.

[12] Brueggemann, First and Second Samuel, p. 26.

[13] Harper's Bible Commentary, p. 270.

[14] Hertzberg, p. 35.

[15] Ibid., p. 150.

[16] Baldwin, p. 87.

[17] Brueggemann, First and Second Samuel, pp. 98, 99. Brueggemann wonders if Samuel came to the camp already prepared to reject Saul (p. 100), but if the prophet was so hostile, he would not have later grieved over the king's fate (1 Sam. 15:35; 16:1; cf. 1 Sam. 15:10, 11 in which the prophet becomes angry and frustrated when God expresses disappointment at choosing Saul). Samuel cries to God all night. Did Samuel try to change God's mind about Saul?

[18] Ibid., p. 99.

[19] Ibid.

[20] Hertzberg, p. 106.

[21] Ibid.

[22] International Standard Bible Encyclopedia, vol. 3, p. 416; vol. 4, p. 338.

[23] Baldwin, p. 127.

[24] Combat between two champions was a Greek custom that the Philistines had carried from their homeland.

[25] A fact that often surfaces in later stories about David and his struggles to protect his throne.

[26] Baldwin, p. 127.

[27] Brueggemann, First and Second Samuel, p. 132.

[28] Donald J. Wiseman, 1 & 2 Kings: An Introduction and Commentary (Leicester, Eng.: InterVarsity Press, 1993), p. 198.

[29] Most probably some kind of skin disease rather than what we know as leprosy today (Hansen's disease).

[30] Katharine Doob Sakenfeld, Ruth (Louisville, Ky.: John Knox Press, 1999), p. 79.

[31] Ibid.

[32] Also called Joash.

[33] Interestingly, 2 Kings says almost the same thing about Hezekiah (2 Kings 18:5).

CHAPTER 8

Helping One Another

ॐ

The harsh conditions of the biblical world made people totally dependent on each other. Loners could not survive. Like the pioneers on the American frontier, everyone would pitch in when someone needed help. The universal understanding was that I will help you and you will return the favor in my time of need. Many of the laws of the Old Testament reinforced the responsibility that the Israelites felt for one another. The Bible calls it hospitality, a concept we have mentioned elsewhere. Hospitality is far more than inviting someone over for a meal. It is assisting others in every aspect of life, no matter what their need might be.

During New Testament times the early Christians supported each other not only spiritually and emotionally but also materially. This was especially important if a believer's family had disowned him or her. Only a few ways of earning a living existed outside the extended family circle. During Old Testament times most people lived in small villages and managed family farms. By New Testament times, more people lived in impersonal cities. A small privileged class controlled most of the wealth. In many ways it was more difficult for the average person to survive than hundreds of years before. The church became the believer's new family, aiding and encouraging the convert.

During Christ's life on earth this ingrained concern for others manifested itself in a new way. Many people helped needy individuals come to Christ for physical and spiritual healing. After His death His followers added witnessing to their sense of social responsibility. They spread the news of salvation through the death and resurrection of Christ, demonstrating the ancient concept of hospitality in the context of Christian love.[1] The church grew because its members brought others to the Christian community. Evangelism was caring for others in its highest form.

In every era, unfortunately, some also fail their social and spiritual responsibilities. We will look at examples of those who shared true concern for their fellow human beings and of some who did not live up to their God-given duties.

The Paralytic and His Friends

In a world without special social programs to assist the blind, the crippled, and others with special problems, family and friends had to meet the needs of such individuals. While most earned their living by begging—the welfare program of the ancient world—people would help them in other ways. The paralyzed man whose story appears in three of the Gospels (Matt. 9:2-7; Mark 2:3-12; and Luke 5:18-25) was fortunate to have several good friends to aid him. Mark mentions four of them. Learning that Jesus had returned to Capernaum, they brought their paralyzed friend to Him to see if the many accounts of Jesus' healing ability were true. Perhaps He could restore the man to a normal life. But when they reached where Jesus was staying, they discovered that the little house had become so crowded that no one else could get in. That did not stop them, however. If they could not bring their friend to Jesus through the door, they would find another way.

Palestinian houses often had stairways going up the outside wall to the roof. People worked on the flat roofs, stored things there, and often slept on them during hot weather. Because wood was scarce—especially timbers long enough to frame a roof—builders constructed the roofs from a few beams covered with a layer of branches or thatch. Then they spread mud and clay over the branches and packed it down with a stone roller. If the roof began to leak during the rainy season, the householder would fill the eroded spot with more clay, tamp it down, and run the stone roller over it.

Thus it was quite easy for the paralyzed man's friends to

break through the layer of clay with a wooden shovel or other tool (Mark 2:4),[2] remove some of the branches, and lower the man between the few larger beams. They eased the man down on a sleeping mat suspended by ropes.

One wonders what the occupants of the house must have thought as dirt and other debris began to rain down on their heads. Jesus probably smiled to Himself at the friends' devotion and ingenuity. He admired their faith (Matt. 9:2; Mark 2:5; Luke 5:20). Christ recognized that the paralyzed man seemed more concerned about spiritual forgiveness than physical healing, since people of his time saw illness and disability of any kind as punishment for sin.[3] Before doing anything else Jesus told him that his sins were forgiven.

A number of scribes and Pharisees had crowded into the room. Jesus' statement that the disabled man's sins were forgiven angered them, and they began to accuse Christ of blasphemy, the defamation of God's name and character (Matt. 9:3; Mark 2:7; Luke 5:21). Since Scripture prescribed elaborate rituals of atonement, and forgiveness was a divine prerogative, for Jesus to forgive the man by mere words shocked the religious leaders.[4] Only God could forgive sins (Mark 2:7; Luke 5:21), and they saw Jesus as usurping the Lord's rightful role. To show that He had authority to forgive sins, Jesus told the paralyzed man to stand up, pick up the mat his friends had lowered him into the house on—and which was a symbol of his condition—and go home (Matt. 9:5-8; Mark 2:8-12; Luke 5:22-26). The mat was now something to sleep on, not to be carried on.

The friends, who showed the true biblical principle of hospitality, of caring for their fellow human beings, had obtained not only physical healing for the man but spiritual healing as well.

Healing at a Pagan Shrine

While the paralyzed man in Capernaum had friends to care for him, the invalid at the pool of Bethesda (or Beth-zatha) had no one to help him.[5] Whether he had family to bring him food or he survived by begging we do not know. Clearly he spent most of his time alone. In his case biblical society had failed much of its responsibility.

The pool he lay beside was most likely the one archaeologists have excavated north of the Temple area near the Sheep Gate and now near the Crusader-built Church of St. Anne. The name Beth-zatha may have come from the northern suburb that it was located in. The pool was a kind of spa that the local inhabitants began to view as a place of healing (John 5:3).[6] Archaeological evidence suggests that the pool (probably originally known as the Sheep Pool) may have contained a shrine to one of the pagan gods of healing, such as Serapis or Asclepius. Excavations have uncovered votive offerings in the ruins similar to those offered to such gods elsewhere. When the Romans rebuilt Jerusalem as the pagan city they called Aelia Capitolina after 135 A.D., the site became an official Roman cultish place of healing.

A portico—a roofed walkway structure supported by pillars—lined the sides of the pool. A thick retaining wall divided the pool into two sections, and a fifth portico covered it. Occasional changes in the flow of water into the pool—perhaps through a conduit connecting the two pools—would disturb the surface of the water. A superstition developed that an angel ruffled the water (verse 7), and that the first person who slipped into the water after it became agitated would be healed.

The sick man had waited beside the pool for 38 years (verse 5), a period longer than the entire life span of most people during the New Testament era. Whatever family he had must have died off long before. Seeing him one day, Jesus asked the man if he wanted to be made well (verse 6). The invalid explained that he had no one to help him into the water—that someone else always got in first (verse 7). He thought only of being cured in the waters of the pool. Jesus then tells him to pick up his sleeping mat and walk. The man did so, and received healing (verse 9).

For nearly four decades the people of Jerusalem had given the sick man only minimal care. Unfortunately the compassion did not improve after his healing. Because Jesus had healed him on Sabbath, a number of religious leaders accosted him and accused him of breaking the Sabbath regulations by carrying his sleeping mat (verse 10). Probably still in a state of shock from being healed, he tried to explain that he was only doing what the Person who had healed him had told him to do (verse 11). The religious leaders knew who had performed the miracle, but wanted the former invalid to verify that Jesus had been the one. They sought to use the incident of alleged Sabbathbreaking to drive a wedge between Jesus and the people. It did not matter to them that Jesus had helped the man—had shown true hospitality, something they should have done. Now the religious leaders were using the Sabbath as an excuse to continue to ignore their responsibility toward the man.

Jesus responded to the accusation about Sabbathbreaking by declaring, "My Father is still working, and I also am working" (verse 17). He cared for and helped His creation just as the Father did. But by implication the religious leaders were not fulfilling their responsibility toward their fellow human beings.

Jesus had been the sick man's friend and helper even when his fellow human beings paid no attention to him. All those who follow Jesus will reflect His care and concern for others. But that compassion involves more than meeting physical, economic, or social needs. God's people will seek to bring others to Him, incorporating them into the community of faith, as we see in an experience among Jesus' first few disciples.

"Come and See"

God seeks only rarely to draw people to Himself through miracles or other dramatic events. He prefers to work through human beings. Skeptics can explain away unusual phenomena or question its meaning, but a consistent demonstration of a transformed life is much harder to ignore.

In John 1 Jesus' cousin John the Baptist proclaims Jesus as the Lamb of God to two of the prophet's own disciples (John 1:36). It is a directive for them to follow Jesus. John wants all his disciples to join Jesus.[7] The Baptist introduced and recommended them to Him even though he knew that they would leave him. But he was willing to decrease, to lose his influence and disciples, that Jesus might increase (John 3:25-30). The two men literally followed after Jesus (John 1:37). They spent the day talking with Him. What He said to them clearly impressed the two men so much that they wanted to share their discovery with others.

One of John's disciples was Andrew, Simon Peter's brother.[8] Andrew wants to introduce his brother to the wonderful experience that has so quickly transformed his life, and soon brings him to Jesus (verse 42). Our relationship with Jesus can survive only when shared. It cannot be hidden and still be expected to grow.

The next day Jesus summons Philip to follow Him (verse 43), and the pattern of sharing continues. It cannot be otherwise. A person in love wants to tell others about it. Newly married people try to convince others about the wonder and joy of marriage. The advice columnist Ann Landers once wrote that the hardest part of having an extramarital affair is that those involved can't tell everybody about it as much as they might want to. Love is meant to be shared. Philip rushes to Nathanael, declaring, "We have found him about whom Moses in the law and also the prophets wrote, Jesus son of Joseph from Nazareth" (verse 45).

Jesus preferred to let others witness for Him for several reasons. First, as we have already mentioned, personal testimony is more convincing to most people than dramatic events or even miracles. We inherently trust the word of those we are close to. Second, when we personally witness to others about God we bond to them. We become brothers and sisters to them within the church family. Such spiritual and emotional ties motivate us to care for others and to help them in times of need. They are also less likely to leave the church, because they feel a strong sense of belonging, of community, and of identity. Members with many close friends in the church have an awareness of being part of something larger than themselves. When crises strike, they have emotional and spiritual as well as physical resources to draw upon. Research studies have found that if new members do not find such friends and relationships within a few months after joining, they will drift away.

Also, God wants to reveal what He is like through the transformations He works in our lives. When we reach out to others, we portray how God seeks to restore all humanity to the family of God. They can also observe in us what He longs to do in their lives. But God can work through us only as we develop a trusting and loyal relationship with Him. We must have what Scripture calls faith. An incident in Mark 9 depicts both what can happen when we establish such a relationship and the dangers of forgetting or failing to maintain it.

Father of Faith, Disciples of Doubt

Many people equate faith with intellectual belief. They often assume that faith is believing something no matter what. Malina and Rohrbaugh comment that at least in the English-speaking world "faith or belief usually means a psychological, internal, cognitive, and affective assent of mind to truths. This assent is given either because the truths make sense in themselves (e.g., most people believe if A = C and B = C, then A = B) or because the person speaking has credibility (e.g., most college students simply 'believe' the authors of their chemistry and physics textbooks about the outcome of experiments mentioned since there is no time in college to replicate all the experiments). This dimension of faith, assent to something or to something somebody says, is not common in the New Testament."[9]

Such a concept of faith as belief in an intellectual concept can be carried to an extreme. That is, the more improbable something seems, the greater our faith if we believe it anyway. But a careful reading of Scripture reveals that the core of true biblical faith is trusting in Jesus and what He will do for us. Even more than that, faith is a relationship with Him. Malina and Rohrbaugh remind us that most frequently "the words 'faith,' 'have faith,' and 'believe' refer in the New Testament to the social glue that binds one person to another. They point to the social, externally manifested, emotional behavior of loyalty, commitment, and solidarity. . . . Jesus requires loyalty and commitment to himself and his project."[10] Faith is not what we believe but whom we believe. Christian faith is dedicating our life to Jesus, following Him, and doing what He says. It is trusting in what He can do, not in how well we can believe.

We see this principle in operation in Mark 9:14-29. Jesus returns from the Mount of Transfiguration to find a crowd, and some scribes arguing with them (verse 14). When He asks what the commotion is about, a father explains that he has brought his son to the disciples to have him exorcized of a demon, but the disciples have failed (verses 16-18). Christ has a definite reason for having the father explain his problem. "The Lord is not just interested in a 'case history' of the boy. He is making the man confess how desperate his case is—making, as it were, faith as difficult as possible for him, and at the same time showing him that he has no other resource but the Christ."[11]

The crowd brings the boy to Jesus. As they do so the demon throws the lad into a convulsion (verse 20). Jesus inquires how long the son has suffered from such seizures (verse 21). The father explains that they have been happening since childhood. Often they throw him into both fire and water. Then he adds, "If you are able to do anything, have pity on us and help us" (verse 22). Instantly Jesus picks up on the phrase implying doubt of His healing ability—"If you are able"—and replies that all things can be done for those who believe (verse 23).

The issue of faith here does not involve whether the father thinks Jesus has the power to cast out demons but rather whether he trusts Jesus to be the kind of Saviour who will actually do it. Is he willing to commit himself and his son to Jesus?

Each of us may be able to convince ourselves theoretically that God can do something, but that is not biblical faith. We do not yet trust that He will do it in our lives. Nor are we able to take the risk of putting ourselves in His hands. For example, we can believe that some wealthy person is able to give us a million dollars but not expect him or her to hand the money over to us. Faith waits to receive the money. It trusts the person's word and acts accordingly.

The father immediately realizes his lack of trust. He does not try to justify his doubt but says simply, "I believe; help my unbelief" (verse 24). He recognizes that the trust inherent in faith cannot come from himself but is a gift from God (Heb. 12:2). All he can do is to accept that divine gift of faith and then use it. The Holy Spirit convicts us not only of what God can do but, more important, that He will do it for us. We trust His word. In this case the father does more than believe that Jesus is capable of casting out demons. He has to stand back and wait for Him to heal his son.

R. Alan Cole observes of the father, "He had said, 'If you can, help me.' The Lord rebuked his first phrase, and so *with tears* (some manuscripts) the father said, 'Then help me just as I am, a doubter.' In other words, the man was not praying that his unbelief might be 'helped' till it come to the point where it was worthy of meeting with a response from God. We do not need to ask God to increase our faith until it is deserving of salvation, as a sort of 'congruent faith.' That would be justification by works, not justification by faith. Instead, he was asking for practical help, to be demonstrated in the healing of his son, and confessing, deeply moved, that he had nothing to make him worthy of it. His very coming to Christ showed a trembling faith, and this was enough. This is justification by faith." [12]

When the disciples later ask why they have failed to cast out the demon, Jesus says that it is a kind that can be overcome only through prayer (verse 29). They do not yet have the kind of relationship that will enable them to trust Him and allow Him to channel His power through them. The kind of prayer they need appears in the boy's father's prayer. He asks Jesus for help to have confidence in, and be loyal to, God, who alone can overcome the evil forces controlling the son's life. The disciples have begun, after their previous experiences of casting out demons, to assume unconsciously that they have the power within themselves. Sadly, their faith in Jesus is in this instance weaker than the father's.

Earlier, in Mark 8:31-33, Jesus had begun telling the disciples about His coming death and resurrection. Peter had rebuked Him for suggesting such a thing, and Jesus had had to reprimand the disciple. Then He had called the crowd as well as His disciples and had made a powerful allusion to His death by crucifixion (verse 34). Finally, He had taken Peter, James, and John up to a high mountain where He was visited by Moses and Elijah. As they left the mountain, Jesus told the disciples not to speak of the incident until He had risen from the dead (Mark 9:9). It was in this context that Jesus cast out the demon from the boy. Throughout the incident Jesus used resurrection imagery in His healing of the boy (he is dead, he was lifted, or rose, up [verses 26, 27]). As the disciples left after the exorcism, Jesus again tried to tell them about His impending death and resurrection (verses 30, 31). But they did not understand what He meant and were afraid to ask Him about it (verse 32).

The disciples' faith, or trust, in Jesus had been in His miracles and their belief in Him as a Messiah-Deliverer. Now He was trying to lead them to a deeper faith. Jesus was to be the world's redeemer from sin. That salvation would be accomplished on the cross. For the disciples to witness for Him and to represent Him they had to have trust and loyalty (faith) in Him as the resurrected Saviour. After the cross Jesus' death, burial, and resurrection would be the theme of the early church's teaching. It is still the core of Christian teaching today.

Misguided Gatekeepers

Even today childhood is still the most dangerous time of life in many parts of the world. Death statistics tell us that many children do not survive to age 5. As we saw in the previous chapter, it was even worse in the ancient world. Disease, famine, and war struck children first. This very vulnerability caused children to have little status in society. It could even be an insult to be called a child.[13] Sociologists tell us that up to the nineteenth century it was not uncommon for parents to keep an emotional distance from their offspring. One naturally hesitated to get too emotionally attached to one's children when the odds were that the majority of them would not reach adulthood. The emotional attachment would grow as the children managed to survive the diseases and accidents of childhood.

The mothers (and perhaps fathers as well)[14] who brought their children to Jesus in Luke 18:15[15] knew that many of the little ones would die within the next year. Yet they needed the sympathy and caring that they sensed in Jesus. They had come to Jesus for His blessing. To be blessed was to be honored,[16] something that was rare in their lives. Unfortunately, all that the disciples saw was women and children—beings with little status in male-dominated New Testament society—imposing upon Jesus' valuable time and strength. But Jesus wanted the parents to know that He understood their need for empathy and support even if His disciples did not. He would let nothing come between them and Him—not even His most devoted followers. Christ's dedicated representatives can become unwitting barriers between Him and those He seeks to reach. No human being must ever act as a gatekeeper for Christ.

Jesus honored the mothers by honoring their children. Several times in the Gospels He used a child to illustrate the concept of true greatness. In Mark Jesus sat down (the ancient position of authoritative teaching) and summoned the disciples to Him. "'Whoever wants to be first must be last of all and servant of all.' Then he took a little child and put it among them; and taking it in his arms, he said to them, 'Whoever welcomes one such child in my name welcomes me, and whoever welcomes me welcomes not me but the one who sent me'" (Mark 9:35-37; cf. Matt. 18:1-5). If the disciples were to represent and to witness for Him, they must be servants of all as their Master was (Phil. 2:5-11). Even Jesus did not promote Himself, but the Father. Only as His followers become humble can they be exalted. Only then will they be capable of being gateways—not gatekeepers—to Jesus.

Outsiders No Longer

In Matthew 15:21-28 and Mark 7:24-30 the disciples tried to protect Jesus from another class that had little status in their society—Gentiles. A woman comes to Jesus with a request. Matthew calls her a Canaanite woman (Matt. 15:22), a term with even more negative connotations than the Syrophoenician label that Mark uses. The fact that she is a woman adds to the disciples' discomfort. To be seen being followed by a Gentile woman would bring dishonor and reproach upon their Master. They try to get Him to rebuff her. Beyond that, they see the Messiah's mission as limited to their own people, not to the whole world.

It took years for the church to grasp its full mission, as we see in the hesitation of Peter and others to accept Gentiles into the church (Acts 10, 11, 15). For the moment, though, Jesus limited His teaching and healing primarily to Israel (Matt. 15:24; cf. Mark 7:27). Yet even then He was willing to extend His mission beyond His own people. He healed the Roman centurion's servant, observing that the Gentile had greater faith than anyone He had so far encountered in Israel (Matt. 8:5-13). The centurion had great trust in Jesus, as did the woman who now followed behind Jesus and His disciples, shouting her plea for Him to heal her demon-tormented daughter.

When she knelt before Him and begged, "Lord, help me" (Matt. 15:26), He replied, "It is not fair to take the children's food and throw it to the dogs" (verse 26). To be compared to a dog was an even greater insult in the ancient world than it is now. People rarely kept them as pets. Dogs were the half-wild carrion-eaters who prowled the village garbage dump. But she would not be deterred. Her response cleverly defused the potential insult (verse 27). Jesus saw that she had great trust in Him—trust that He was willing to honor. The unnamed woman "is confident that even if she is not entitled to sit down as a guest at the Messiah's table, Gentile 'dog' that she is, yet at least she may be allowed to receive a crumb of the uncovenanted mercies of God. And such humility and faith draw forth the healing power of the Messiah."[17] Jesus exclaims, "'Woman, great is your faith! Let it be done for you as you wish.' And her daughter was healed instantly" (verse 28).

The disciples attempted to keep the Syrophoenician mother away from Jesus because she was a Gentile woman. It did not create a good public image to have her disturbing the Master. Those who told the blind beggar Bartimaeus to be quiet when he shouted "Jesus, Son of David, have mercy on me!" (Mark 10:46-48) also had a public relations reason in mind. The expression "Son of David" had political connotations. The people knew the quickest way to get the Roman authorities down on them was to make public references to the Jewish national dynasty. To the Romans the beggar would be shouting for a political pretender and potential revolutionary. They would consider it an act of rebellion. The phrase alluded to the story of David returning to claim his kingdom recorded in 2 Samuel 19:31-20:3.[18]

But Jesus, who would not allow indifference to children or ethnic prejudice to come between Him and those He wanted to bless, heal, or save, also condemned those who would let political fear serve as a barrier between Him and anyone. He wanted His disciples to bring others to Him, not hinder or block their access. And He wanted His followers to demonstrate in their own lives the kind of loyalty and trust He desired.

---

[1] For the theme of hospitality in the Bible and early Christianity, see C. Pohl, *Making Room;* Gerald Wheeler, *Beyond Life,* pp. 31-34; David L. Balch, *Families in the New Testament World: Households and House Churches* (Louisville: Westminster John Knox, 1997).

[2] The Greek of Mark 2:4 reads literally that as they began "digging through" they "unroofed the roof where he [Jesus] was" (Robert A. Guelich, *Mark 1-8:26,* Word Biblical Commentary [Dallas: Word Books, 1989], vol. 34a, p. 85). Interestingly, Luke has the men lowering the paralytic "through the tiles," a type of roof construction that would be more familiar to readers elsewhere in the Roman Empire, especially urban areas (John Nolland, *Luke 1-9:20,* Word Biblical Commentary [Dallas: Word Books, 1989], vol. 35a, p. 234).

[3] See, for example, the disciple's question about the man blind from birth in John 9:1-3.

[4] *Harper's Bible Commentary,* p. 988.

[5] *Anchor Bible Dictionary,* vol. 1, p. 701.

[6] *Harper's Bible Commentary,* p. 1054.

[7] George R. Beasley-Murray, *John* (Word Biblical Commentary, vol. 36) (Waco, Tex.: Word Books, 1987), p. 26.

[8] The other, unnamed, disciple has been variously identified as the Beloved Disciple or Philip. Beasley-Murray suggests Philip because the book of John elsewhere associates him with Andrew *(ibid.).*

[9] B. Malina and R. Rohrbaugh, *Synoptic Gospels,* p. 252.

[10] *Ibid.*

[11] R. Alan Cole, *The Gospel According to St. Mark: An Introduction and Commentary* (Leicester, Eng.: InterVarsity Press, 1961), p. 146.

[12] *Ibid.,* p. 147.

[13] Malina and Rohrbaugh, *Synoptic Gospels,* p. 238.

[14] Leon Morris suggests that since the pronoun translated "them" is masculine, fathers may have accompanied the mothers and children (Leon Morris, *Luke,* p. 291).

[15] Luke calls them "infants," making them of even less status in ancient society since they were much more vulnerable to death.

[16] Malina and Rohrbaugh, *Synoptic Gospels,* p. 47.

[17] R.V.G. Trasker, *The Gospel According to St. Matthew: An Introduction and Commentary* (Leicester, Eng.: InterVarsity Press, 1961), p. 152.

[18] *Harper's Bible Commentary,* p. 998.

CHAPTER 9

The Intercessors

Prayer is ultimately a mystery. It raises questions that seem to have no easy answers—if there are any answers at all. Why does God seem to intervene more when we ask than when we don't? Why pray at all? Doesn't He already know better than we do what we need? Does prayer somehow permit Him freedom in a Satan-dominated world? Is prayer for God's benefit—or ours? How does intercessory prayer really work?

We do not understand prayer, but Scripture and experience teach us that it is a powerful form of communication with God. The apostle Paul tells us to make our requests known to God (Phil. 4:6). John says that if we ask according to God's will and in His name He will hear us and answer (1 John 5:14, 15; John 14:13, 14). James especially urges believers to pray. "Are any among you suffering? They should pray. . . . Are any among you sick? They should call for the elders of the church and have them pray over them. . . . The prayer of faith will save the sick. . . . Pray for one another, so that you may be healed. The prayer of the righteous is powerful and effective" (James 5:13-16). Prayer is not just for ourselves but also for others (2 Cor. 9:14; 13:7; 2 Thess. 1:11; 3:1; Heb. 13:18).

Biblical prayers go far beyond the pagan petitions preserved in ancient scrolls, tablets, and monumental inscriptions.[1] Egyptian and Mesopotamian prayers tended to be favors begged, negotiated, or obtained by flattery or bribery from impersonal and distant deities. There is little intimacy between the one who prays and the god.[2] But the God of the Bible not only listens to and grants human requests; He responds to humanity as one person to another. The people of the Bible offer their prayers in the context of a personal relationship with God Himself. And prayer is more than just asking for something. It is speaking to God, thanking Him, praising Him, opening ourselves up to Him. True prayer is not a one-way conversation. We must listen as well as talk.

People in Scripture prayed both for themselves and for others. We will look at examples of each.

"Remember Now, O Lord"

The story of Hezekiah is especially interesting in that it is one of several that show God honoring requests that go contrary to His previously expressed will. The Lord announces through the prophet Isaiah that the king would die (2 Kings 20:1; cf. Isa. 38). The death is not a punishment or judgment on Hezekiah.[3] Scripture regards him as an exceptionally good king (2 Kings 18:3; 2 Chron. 31:20, 21). He faces death simply because he lives in a world full of sickness. Since the story is set in the context of the siege of Jerusalem, and disease almost always breaks out both in the besieging army and among the besieged because of large numbers of people brought together in unsanitary conditions, one wonders if there is a connection between the siege and the king's illness. Whatever the cause of the king's condition, he has a fatal illness and must deal with that fact. Isaiah's command to "set your house in order" may include selecting a successor.[4]

Naturally, Hezekiah finds his impending fate difficult to accept. Turning his face to the wall in an attempt to find some privacy, he prays, "Remember now, O Lord, I implore you, how I have walked before you in faithfulness with a whole heart, and have done what is good in your sight" (2 Kings 20:3). The king reminds God of his faithful life, using phraseology that the author of Kings reserves for those that the two books present as the better rulers of Judah. "Hezekiah's claim to virtue is in no way presumptuous; he follows accepted prayer practice in asserting his own righteousness (Ps. 17:3-5; 26:1-5). Tears underscore his sincerity and desperation (Ps. 6:6; 39:12)."[5] The king does not directly ask for a reprieve, only that God not forget how he has served Him.

Isaiah has barely left the palace before the Lord sends a message to the prophet. He tells Isaiah to return and report to the king that He has heard Hezekiah's prayer and will heal him. In fact, He will add 15 years to the king's life. It is equivalent to more than half a life span when one remembers that life expectancy for most people in the ancient Near East at this period was around 20 years. Fifteen years would have allowed a successor who was still an infant to reach what the Old Testament regarded as adulthood. Besides that, Isaiah says, God will defend Jerusalem from the invading Assyrian forces "for my [God's] sake and for my servant David's sake" (2 Kings 20:4-6). When the king asks for assurance that God will indeed spare him, the Lord makes the shadow of a sundial (most likely a stair-steplike structure) move backward 10 degrees (verses 8-11).

Many commentators have suggested that Hezekiah should not have asked God for extended life, especially in light of his flaunting the royal treasures of Judah before the delegation from Babylonia (verses 12-19).[6] Second Chronicles 32:25 declares that "Hezekiah did not respond according to the benefit done to him, for his heart was proud." He came to realize his mistake, but the damage was already done, though God graciously held back the consequences until after the king's death (verse 26).

Did the Lord prolong Hezekiah's life just to show that the king would use his extra years foolishly, as some suggest? Does God play games with us? Perhaps it would be best just to say that if God honors our prayers, He then lets us decide whether we will use His answers wisely or squander them. The king may have made a mistake later, but he was not predestined to do it. Hezekiah's response to Isaiah's announcement of the king's death was sincere. God does not give us something just to demonstrate that we will abuse it. Human parents may play such tricks to prove a point, but God does not mock us. When He grants our prayers, it is always our responsibility to use those answers wisely and to His glory. It is the same with every blessing He gives.

"Have Mercy on Me, O God"

Bible readers idealize David, ignoring the great shadows in his life. But the Bible does not hide the fact that he was far from perfect. The biblical records show many weaknesses and failings. Even on his deathbed he plotted with his son Solomon the fate of his rivals and enemies (1 Kings 2:5-9). But when God confronted him about his sins, David was willing to acknowledge them—something too few human beings are willing to do. God can forgive us only when we recognize the need for forgiveness. The Lord can heal us only when we admit our spiritual sickness and bring it to Him. David may often have been a great sinner, but he was an even greater repenter. When faced with his sins, he would bow in submission to God and with a broken heart plead for forgiveness.

The heading of Psalm 51 presents it as a prayer that David made after the incident with Bathsheba recorded in 2 Samuel 11 and 12. The prophet Nathan confronted the king with what he had done, and David acknowledged his sin. Psalm 51 depicts the kind of prayers he must have said as in agony he pleaded for God's forgiveness. It is one of seven penitential psalms in the book of Psalms (Ps. 6, 32, 38, 51, 102, 130, 143). It contains "a full confession of sin which is without parallel in any other biblical psalm." [7]

In the psalm David does not approach God from his position as king (as pagan rulers would have done)[8] or from any righteousness he might have, but seeks God's great mercy (Ps. 51:1). He acknowledges his true nature as a sinner and his need for spiritual cleansing (verses 2, 3, 7, 10). Although he committed adultery with Bathsheba, caused the death of her husband Uriah the Hittite, and had considered himself above human and divine law, thus shattering the trust of his people, his sin—as is the case with all sin—was ultimately against God (verse 4). David knew that only God could make a lasting transformation in his life. The Lord must continually sustain him (verse 12). The only thing any sinner can offer God is a broken spirit, a broken and contrite heart (verse 17), and even that is a gift from God Himself when He puts "a new and right spirit within" the repentant sinner (verse 10).

Here we find the fundamental difference between David and

his predecessor, Saul. Saul's sins (excluding the incident at Endor) were far less serious than David's, but he refused to acknowledge or face up to them. David might sin more deeply, but he also repented more deeply. Despite all his faults David would always return to an intimate relationship with God.

"Save My People"

Intercessory is one of the most important kinds of prayer. We first see it in Genesis 18, in which God pronounces judgment on Sodom and Gomorrah. When He tells Abraham what He plans to do, the patriarch pleads for Him to spare the cities if they have at least a minimum number of righteous people living in them. In typical Near Eastern fashion Abraham bargains with God, bringing that number down successively from 50 to 10. God takes his intercession seriously. Although the doomed cities do not have even the agreed-upon minimum number of righteous, the Lord respects Abraham's intervention for Sodom and Gomorrah. Again He is not playing games with the patriarch's intercessory prayer.

God also regards with utmost respect Moses' intercessory prayer in Exodus 32. Once more we see someone asking the Lord to change His already-announced intentions.

The Israelites have demonstrated their distrust of Moses and God by creating a golden calf. They want a god they can see, the kind that they knew in Egypt and that other Semitic peoples worshiped. The Hebrews did not completely reject the God of Abraham, Isaac, and Jacob—Aaron proclaimed that the next day "shall be a festival to the Lord" (Ex. 32:5)—but they wanted to depict their divine leading in ways familiar to them from the pagan world around them. R. Alan Cole suggests that the golden calf was the Canaanite Baal that was also worshiped in the Nile delta.[9] God's people mingled false worship with the true. They bowed down to Yahweh as just one God among many and seemed unable to grow beyond what they had known when He led them out of Egypt. His people had repeatedly complained and questioned Him since their deliverance. Now He tells Moses that He has had enough.

The people, as they demand that Aaron make them gods, declare that Moses has been the one who led them out from Egypt (Ex. 32:1). God, who knows what they are doing and saying, tells Moses, who is on the mountain with Him, "Go down at once! *Your* people, whom *you have brought up out of the land of Egypt,* have acted perversely" (verse 7). "I have seen this people, how stiff-necked they are," God continues. "Now let me alone, so that my wrath may burn hot against them and I may consume them; and of you I will make a great nation" (verses 9, 10).

What God meant by saying that He would "consume" them we cannot be sure. But Terence E. Fretheim suggests that Exodus 34:7 and 32:33 may offer some clues. He sees the threatened action to be not a sudden annihilation but an isolation from God's special care and concern. It would allow the "brokenness" to have its effect on them. "In other words, Israel is staring into the face of a future far more devastating than any experience of bondage in Egypt."[10]] God will leave them to the consequences of their continuing wrong decisions. He will give them what they want—to their eventual destruction.

The Lord's offer to make a mighty nation of Moses' descendants must have been tempting. Israel had given their human leader nothing but grief. Perhaps Moses' own family could do better (but consider the behavior of Miriam and Aaron). The people would bear the name "sons of Moses" instead of "sons of Israel." But Moses would not let go of them. As Abraham had long before interceded for Sodom and Gomorrah, he would now intercede for Israel.

The fact that God said "Let me alone" indicates that the divine decision was not yet fixed. "For such a word to make sense, one must assume that, while God has decided to execute wrath (see verse 14), the decision has not reached an irretrievable point; the will of God is not set on the matter. Moses could conceivably contribute something to the divine deliberation that might occasion a future for Israel other than wrath. In fact, God seems to anticipate that Moses will resist what is being said. At the least, it recognizes that what Moses might say about God's decision places some limits on what it might be possible for God to do. God here recognizes the relationship with Moses over having an absolutely free decision in this matter. The devastation of Israel by the divine wrath is thus conditioned upon Moses giving God leave to do so. While the reader cannot hear the tone of the remark, 'Let me alone,' it may well refer to the isolation desired to suffer grief. But God thereby does leave the door of Israel's future open."[11]

One gets the distinct feeling that God wants Moses to talk Him out of abandoning Israel. Either we take the incident seriously and at face value, or we have to dismiss it as some kind of game God is playing with Moses, that He does not really mean what He is saying.

Moses resists the temptation to let the difficult people of Israel go their own way, and pleads for them (verses 11-13). He appeals to:

1. God's reasonableness.
2. God's reputation.
3. God's own promise.

Obviously, the Lord has already considered each point Moses brings up. But for the Hebrew leader to argue them gives them new meaning or status. "God is open to what Moses has to say and takes Moses' contribution with utmost seriousness, honoring it as an important ingredient for the shaping of the future. If Moses wills and thinks and does these things, they take on a significance that they do not carry when treated in divine isolation. It is not a matter of Moses' winning the argument but of a relationship that God takes seriously."[12]

Exodus 32:14 declares that "the Lord changed his mind about the disaster that he planned to bring on his people."[13] Cole believes that such passages as this mean that God now embarks on a different course than what He had previously stated, because of "some new factor which is usually mentioned in the context. In the Bible, it is clear that God's promises and warnings are always conditional on man's response: this is most clearly set out in Ezekiel 33:13-16."[14] God chooses to involve humanity in His work and sometimes even in His decisions.

The incident raises many questions in our minds. Some have seen God as just testing Moses to see how he would react. But we have already rejected the idea that a loving God plays games with His creation. Was He thundering destruction to scare Israel into behaving? Everyday life reminds us that fear will not permanently change anybody for the better. Or was God helping Moses to experience God's own love for Israel by allowing him to intercede for his people? Was He letting Moses know what it means to be an intercessor and thus provide a living example of the mystery and power of intercessory prayer? Intercessory prayer that all believers have the privilege of participating in? And was Moses' prayer a type of Jesus' intercession in heaven?

In the end we must admit that we cannot explain all the reasons and details of intercessory prayer. We can only acknowledge and perform it. God invites us to intercede for others, and we must accept the divine calling.

"We Have Sinned"

Daniel's prayer in Daniel 9 is another powerful illustration of how God longs for us to intercede for both ourselves and others. God's people are now in exile, and the prophet struggles with the fear and concern that it might be a permanent situation. Jeremiah had prophesied that Israel would remain in exile for 70 years, then God would bring them back (Jer. 29:1-14). But would God really fulfill His promise? The exiles' situation seems no different than it has been for decades.

The prophet decides to pray about the crucial question. He first prepares himself spiritually by fasting and wearing sackcloth and ashes (Dan. 9:3). Prayer of any kind is not something we should do lightly, especially intercessory prayer. When we pray we are speaking to the powerful God of the universe, and while He is a loving and promisekeeping deity, prayer is a serious thing. After acknowledging God's awesome nature, Daniel clearly states that Israel has sinned. The prophet includes himself with his people: "We have sinned and done wrong, acted wickedly and rebelled, turning aside from your commandments and ordinances. We have not listened to your servants the prophets, who spoke in your name to our kings, our princes, and our ancestors, and to all the people of the land" (verses 5, 6; cf. verses 11, 15).

Even though he is a prophet himself, Daniel identifies with the rest of God's people. He regards himself as a part of the community of faith, thus sharing in both their strengths and their failures. Those who intercede with God feel an intimate relationship with the ones they pray for. Moses, when he pleaded for his people a second time, would rather have been blotted out himself than to see his people lost (Ex. 32:32). Jesus demonstrated the conviction of His intercessory prayers by His death on the cross. To pray for another is to love and care for that person with a depth and intensity that God and His people alone can know.

One of the fundamental characteristics of sin is that it wants to deny any responsibility for its actions. As representative of his people, Daniel confesses that he and his people have rebelled and now are reaping the consequences that God had warned them about in the book of Deuteronomy ("the law of Moses") (verse 11). He admits that God is righteous in all that He does and that His people deserve their exile (verse 7). Israel has not obeyed His word or listened to His spokespersons. Daniel and his people have become a disgrace to God (verse 16).

As we have recognized before, God cannot help those who have no problems. But Daniel acknowledges that he and his people have done wrong and need divine aid. He appeals for such deliverance, not on the basis of their righteousness but on God's great mercy (verse 18). Only His love and unmerited grace assure salvation. No one is ever saved because they are good—only because God is good.

When we pray for others, we must also recognize our own need. Often God may use us to answer those prayers. But He can work most fully through us only as we are willing to let Him transform us into willing and able agents of His mission on earth. Reformation and renewal begin with those who first ask for it, whether it be great leaders such as Daniel or the lowliest members of God's family. When we pray for others, we are at the same time praying for ourselves.

Peter at the Door

When we think of prayer we usually have in mind individuals praying, either by themselves or as representatives of a group, such as the pastoral prayer in a church service. Too often we have been oblivious of the need for, and the power in, group or corporate prayer. As we pray together we strengthen each other. We encourage and uphold each one. Even Jesus in Gethsemane longed for the support of His disciples when He prayed for strength to face His approaching death (Matt. 26:36-41; Mark 14:32-38). Although He was doing the praying, He still wanted the encouragement of their presence.

After they found themselves forced out of the synagogues, early Christian congregations met in private homes. Church buildings would not become common for hundreds of years. Home churches provided worship and other religious services with an intimacy too often lacking in formal church buildings. The members met as an extended family. They were not spectators, passively listening to some official preach or pray. The small rooms of private homes brought them emotionally and spiritually as well as physically close. Today small cell groups within a larger congregation are seeking to recapture the flavor of early Christian worship.

Herod Agrippa I, the grandson of Herod the Great, acquired a steadily growing kingdom from the emperors Gaius and Claudius. By A.D. 41 his rule extended over an area comparable to that of the first Herod. Perhaps learning from the mistakes of his grandfather, he sought to win the favor of his people, especially the Pharisees who had fought Herod the Great. As part of that attempt to gain their support, Herod Agrippa began to attack the growing Christian community. He had James the brother of John executed (Acts 12:2) and arrested Peter, putting him under heavy guard in prison (verses 3, 4). Four squads of soldiers guarded this one man. At night they bound him with two chains, and he had to sleep between two soldiers. More guards remained on duty in front of the prison door. The tight security made his eventual escape only more dramatic.

The Jerusalem community immediately began to pray for Peter (verse 5). "It was fervent prayer which was offered, like that offered by Jesus in Gethsemane (Luke 22:44), expressive of the church's concern for Peter rather than of a feeling that, if God is to answer prayer, he must be pressed and persuaded by spectacular feats of devotion."[15] The prayer continued for several days.[16]

God may have in part permitted Peter's imprisonment, not only to show His power to deliver but also to bring the Christian community closer together. Peter's jailing united them in a common concern and goal. When the angel freed Peter, he headed to the home of Mary, the mother of John Mark. There he found many believers praying (Acts 12:12). Because people normally went to bed soon after it became dark, it is significant that church members would go to the expense of lighting the little clay oil lamps and remain awake to pray.

"The body of believers, by praying for one another," John Sanders observes, "helps to shape the future of the community. What God decides to do for others sometimes seems to depend on my prayers. That is, God might sometimes refrain from acting beneficially in one person's life because others have failed to pray. This may not sound fair to those of us in the West with our high values of individualism, but God values community and desires that it be fostered, in part, by our concern for one another and by our manifesting this concern in intercessory prayer for others. This is one means that God uses to build a community of fellowship and mutual concern."[17]

---

[1] See, for example, the samples in *Hymns, Prayers, and Songs: An Anthology of Ancient Egyptian Lyric Poetry,* trans. John L. Foster (Atlanta: Scholars Press, 1995). Other sources of ancient prayers include J. B. Pritchard, ed., *Ancient Near Eastern Texts Relating to the Old Testament,* and D. Winton Thomas, *Documents From Old Testament Times.* They will give a flavor of how other cultures prayed to their gods.

[2] One does at times find a personal relationship between the one who prays and the god, but it is not as pervasive as in the Bible. See, for example, *Letters*

From Ancient Egypt, p. 10.

[3] Richard Nelson, *First and Second Kings* (Atlanta: John Knox Press, 1987), p. 243.

[4] D. Wiseman, *1 & 2 Kings,* p. 286.

[5] Nelson, p. 244.

[6] The delegation from Marduk-apla-iddinna II may have been seeking to arrange an anti-Assyrian alliance (Wiseman, p. 288). Such an alliance would have demonstrated a lack of faith in God's power to protect Jerusalem, as well as involving Judah in pagan politics, a problem that intensified among the later kings of Judah (see the book of Jeremiah).

[7] Marvin E. Tate, *Psalms 51-100,* Word Biblical Commentary (Dallas: Word Books, 1990), vol. 20, p. 8.

[8] In Egypt, the pharaoh was a fellow god.

[9] R. Alan Cole, *Exodus: An Introduction and Commentary* (Downers Grove, Ill.: InterVarsity Press, 1973), p. 214.

[10] Terence E. Fretheim, *Exodus* (Louisville, Ky.: John Knox Press, 1991), p. 284.

[11] *Ibid.,* pp. 283, 284.

[12] *Ibid.,* p. 286.

[13] Moses would intercede for his people twice more (Ex 32:30-34 and 34:8, 9).

[14] Cole, p. 217.

[15] I. Howard Marshall, *The Acts of the Apostles: An Introduction and Commentary* (Leicester, Eng.: InterVarsity Press, 1980), p. 208.

[16] *Ibid.*

[17] J. Sanders, *The God Who Risks,* p. 274.

CHAPTER 10

The Blood of Martyrs

As we read about those who gave their lives for Christ in early church records such as *The History of the Church*, by Eusebius, the suffering they endured both awes and horrifies us. The pagan authorities burned, stoned, and hacked them to death. Wild animals mauled many in public spectacles staged in Roman arenas. Eusebius tells of groups of people leaping onto pyres willingly or declaring themselves Christians after watching the court trials of believers.[1] As the centuries passed it became almost a fad to seek martyrdom. People saw it as a sure guarantee to heaven. But if the word "martyr" means "witness," can someone caught up in mob hysteria or acting on impulse be a true martyr? Can a person witness to a faith he or she barely knows? The Bible depicts martyrs. Are they the same as or do they differ from those of early Christianity?

Strangely, the Bible does not place as much emphasis on martyrdom as does early Christian history. Scripture mentions only a relative few who would come under that category. The first individual that we could classify as a martyr was Abel,[2] but Scripture does not explore why Cain killed him, other than that God "had regard for Abel and his offering, but for Cain and his offering he had no regard" (Gen. 4:4, 5). Cain slew his brother from anger, but the narrator does not explain the motivation behind that anger. Also, both worshiped the Lord, so it was not a case of hostility between different religions.

The King's Mentor

Perhaps a clearer example of what constitutes martyrdom is that of Zechariah, son of the priest Jehoiada. After Jehu had

Ahaziah, king of Judah, put to death (2 Chron. 22:7-9), Ahaziah's mother, Athaliah, seized the throne. The woman was a granddaughter of Omri, king of Israel (verse 2). She and other members of the house of Ahab had persuaded Ahaziah to follow the political and religious practices of the northern kingdom. To prevent any opposition to her seizure of the throne, she had ordered the killing of all the members of the royal house of Judah that she could find. Jehoshabeath, daughter of former king Jehoram, sister of Ahaziah and wife of the priest Jehoiada, managed to escape with her nephew Joash, and hid him in the Temple compound. The child remained in seclusion for six years (verses 10-12). Apparently the queen in her search ignored the Temple precincts.

Then one Sabbath Jehoiada staged a coup against Athaliah and proclaimed the child as king (2 Chron. 23). The priest established a covenant between himself, the people, and the king, that they would be the Lord's people (verse 16). The people then destroyed the temple to Baal that had been set up in Jerusalem and executed its priests (verse 17). The new king, Joash, did much good at first, including the restoration of the neglected Solomonic Temple (2 Chron. 24:1-14). He "did what was right in the sight of the Lord all the days of the priest Jehoiada" (verse 2).

Eventually, Joash's mentor and spiritual guide died (verse 15). The author of Chronicles shows the priest's importance in Judah by describing his death and burial in a way that echoes the passing of kings.[3] Joash now falls under the influence of less faithful officials and counselors. Perhaps out of political motivation they persuaded him to abandon the God of Judah and worship the gods of the surrounding nations (verses 17, 18). God commissioned prophets to call the leadership of Judah back to Him, but to no avail (verse 19).[4]

Then God chose Jehoiada's son Zechariah as His spokesperson (verse 20). The new prophet challenged the people, "Thus says God: Why do you transgress the commandments of the Lord, so that you cannot prosper? Because you have forsaken the Lord, he has forsaken you" (verse 20). Joash's counselors regarded Zechariah as a traitor to the nation and conspired to have him eliminated.[5] At the king's orders Zechariah perished by stoning in the Temple court (verse 21). Years before, Jehoiada had ordered that those involved in the coup against Queen Athaliah not kill her on the Temple grounds so as not to desecrate it (2 Chron. 23:14), but his protegé Joash had no such scruples. The biblical writer condemns Joash, noting that he "did not remember the kindness that Jehoiada, Zechariah's father, had shown him, but killed his son" (2 Chron. 24:22).

As Zechariah died he said, "May the Lord see and avenge" (verse 22). The prophet was "not looking for personal revenge but asking God to act in keeping with his declared principles of justice. If God were inactive, the result would be anarchy, and God's claims to sovereignty would be seriously jeopardized."[6] Jesus would later cite the incident in Matthew 23:29-36 and Luke 11:45-52 as an illustration of the fate awaiting the rebellious leaders of His time.[7] Zechariah's words foreshadow the martyrs of Revelation 6:10, who ask, "Sovereign Lord, holy and true, how long will it be before you judge and avenge our blood on the inhabitants of the earth?"

Sara Japhet points out the lack of proportion between what Zechariah did and his fate. "His brief prophecy was couched in the most general terms, with no specific threats. When compared, for example, with the harsh words of Jeremiah and his contemporaries during the time of the destruction (Jer. 26, etc.), the much earlier prophecy of Amos (Amos 7:7-17), or even the words of Micaiah the son of Imlah (1 Kings 22:28; 2 Chron. 18:27), the unprovocative character of Zechariah's prophecy is all the more obvious. Are these words deserving the death penalty?"[8]

Joash met his own fate within a year. First, the army of Aram attacked Jerusalem and killed the officials who had wrongly advised the king (2 Chron. 24:23). Although the invaders were only a small group, they defeated the much larger forces of Judah, because the Lord "delivered" them into Aram's hands (verse 24).

The battle left Joash wounded. His servants then assassinated him because of what he had done to the son of Jehoiada (verse

25). To dishonor him, they did not bury him in the royal tombs.

The Risky Fate of Prophets

Zechariah was, as we shall continue to see, typical of the biblical martyrs. Such individuals perished because of their systematic defense of true religion and opposition to false worship. The pattern appears in another, though brief, account in Jeremiah 26:20-23, the story of Uriah, son of Shemaiah, from Kiriath-jearim. God sent a message through him identical to that of Jeremiah. But Uriah did not have the influential supporters that Jeremiah had, such as Ahikam, son of Shaphan (verse 24). Uriah's preaching angered the Judahite king Jehoiakim and his supporters, and they sought to kill him.

Both Jeremiah and Uriah protested the various political alliances Judah had been making with neighboring countries. Since the ancient world did not separate religion and state, politics involved religion, and the pagan worship of other nations crept into the royal court of Judah, perhaps as part of the treaties themselves. The prophets of God also proclaimed Judah's approaching destruction and urged the people to submit to Babylon. The alliances had formed in the first place to resist the Neo-Babylonian Empire. How could the Judahite king rally his people's support when Jeremiah and Uriah announced that Judah as a nation was doomed?

Uriah fled to Egypt (verse 21). Jehoiakim dispatched Elnathan, son of Achbor, and a delegation of men to bring Uriah back (verse 22). They, probably with the aid of Egypt, whose envoys were negotiating treaties with Judah against Babylon, captured Uriah and returned him to Jerusalem. There Jehoiakim killed him with the sword and, to show his contempt, had him buried with the common people (verse 23). Apparently Uriah had been a member of the upper class.

John the Baptist

Not all martyrs perished in some dramatic confrontation between God's followers and those of some pagan religion. Their witness did not inspire crowds who became believers through the public spectacle of their death and courage. A person may give his or her life unseen and still be a true martyr. John the Baptist is a classic illustration of those who offered their lives for God behind the scenes.

Although John had preached repentance and reform and the coming of the Messiah, his actual death resulted from his opposition to the marriage of Herod Antipas and his second wife, Herodias. According to Jewish law their relationship was illegal (Mark 6:18). She had previously been married to Herod's brother. Herod Antipas and Herodias divorced their spouses to marry each other. Angry and feeling dishonored, Herod's former father-in-law, the Nabatean king, then invaded and conquered much of Herod's territory. John the Baptist's preaching may thus have sounded like political criticism to Herod,[9] but he hesitated to kill him. Matthew 14:5 suggests that John's popularity held him back,[10] while Mark has Herod protecting him because he "feared John, knowing that he was a righteous and holy man. . . . When he heard him, he was greatly perplexed; and yet he liked to listen to him" (Mark 6:20). Instead he imprisoned him, probably in the desert fortress Machaenus. The prophet's messages, though, especially upset Herodias. Mark 6:19 reports that she held a grudge against John. She got her revenge at Herod's birthday celebration. The drunken king, aroused by the dancing of his stepdaughter Salome, promised her anything she wanted (Matt. 14:7; Mark 6:22). Mark has him offering up to half of his kingdom (Mark 6:23). (Since he was only a Roman vassal, he had no legal right to give away any of his territory.)[11]

Since the fortress Machaenus had separate dining halls for men and women,[12] Salome had to rush to the other hall to ask her mother what she should request (verse 24).[13] Seizing the opportunity, Herodias demanded the head of John the Baptist on a platter—that is, served up as part of the dinner menu, "a ghastly touch of ridicule"[14] toward the man who had pointed out her illicit relationship with Herod. Because he had made his oath in front of his guests and feared that he would lose face if he did not grant Salome what she asked, Herod ordered the execution. Yet the death did in a bizarre way honor the imprisoned prophet. Beheading as a punishment was restricted to Roman citizens and people of higher social status.[15]

John the Baptist died in the gloomy shadows of a dungeon. It was not the kind of death that would inspire his followers. It depressed even Jesus, and He sought to be alone in His grief (Matt. 14:12, 13). The Baptist's death at the hands of a weak but brutal leader foreshadowed Jesus' own fate before Pilate.

History most often focuses on the spectacular. Many martyrs met amazing public deaths. But others witnessed to their faith and the power of God by dying alone. As in the case of others, John's life rather than his death was the greater testimony. He had struggled with crippling doubt (Luke 7:18-20) but he did not give up. And Jesus honored him (verse 28).

Often it seems easier to die for God than to live for Him. How many of those in early church history who sought a martyr's death could have lived the life of true witness that John did?

The First Christian Martyr

Stephen was one of the seven apostolic assistants appointed to help distribute food to the church's poorer members. (Although most Christians think of him as a deacon, Scripture never calls him that.) But his work soon exploded beyond aiding the destitute, as he began to do "great wonders and signs among the people" (Acts 6:8). The power of his preaching and wisdom soon aroused growing opposition (verses 10-12). The religious establishment, seeing him as a growing threat, decided to stop him at any cost. It planted false witnesses to accuse him of speaking blasphemy against Moses and God (verse 11) and to stir up the people against Stephen. Then they seized him and brought him before the Sanhedrin. The religious court interrogated the Christian leader (Acts 6:12-7:1). Stephen defended himself by emphasizing God's warnings about what would happen should His people persist in their disobedience. He began reciting the history of Israel's failures (Acts 7:2-53).

The hostility of his audience soon reached the point at which he had to cut his sermon short. Quickly he summarized his charge that Israel had not really kept God's law as it now claimed. Furious, the mob in the Sanhedrin chambers dragged him outside the city. The rush of the angry crowd to stone him (verse 57) recalls another mob that tried to stone Jesus (John 8:59). But unlike Christ, Stephen would not escape its rage. If, as some scholars suggest, the Sanhedrin met in one of the colonnades on the Temple mount, the mob may have started to parallel Joash's execution of Zechariah on the Temple grounds, though they did carry Stephen outside Jerusalem.

Luke describes Stephen's death in terms that echo Christ's death. Like Jesus, Stephen was innocent, and like Him he offered a prayer of confidence that rephrases Psalm 31:5 (Acts 7:59; cf. Luke 23: 34). The book of Acts sees Stephen's martyrdom as a witness to Christ's death as well as to his faith in his Saviour. Although the death of Stephen has inspired believers through the centuries, it had its most immediate impact on Saul, who would later become Paul the apostle.

"Stretch Out Your Hands"

The apostle Peter denied Jesus three times after vowing that he would go with Him to prison or to the death (Luke 22:33). But after the resurrection Christ, in John 21:15-19, reconciled Peter to the other disciples, who knew of his scandalous behavior, by asking him three times (the same number as the denials) whether he loved Him. Each time Jesus told him to tend or feed His spiritual flocks (verses 15-17). Then Christ added the cryptic statement "Very truly, I tell you, when you were younger, you used to fasten your own belt and to go wherever you wished. But when you grow old, you will stretch out your hands, and someone else will fasten a belt around you and take you where you do not wish to go" (verse 18). John then explained that Christ was foretelling the nature of Peter's death (verse 19). It would "glorify God," a phrase the Gospel used to point to the death of Jesus (John 12:23) and to the Septuagint's description of the death of the suffering servant in Isaiah 52:13. John 21:18, 19 thus provides the first allusion to Peter's eventual martyrdom.

Earlier, in the upper room at the Last Supper, Jesus had told the disciples that He would be leaving them (John 13:33). Peter had asked where He was going (verse 36). Jesus replied, "Where I am going, you cannot follow me now; but you will follow afterward" (verse 36). Demanding to know why he could not accompany his Master, Peter proclaimed, "I will lay down my life for you" (verse 37). At the time Jesus had answered sadly, "Will you lay down your life for me? Very truly, I tell you, before the cock crows, you will have denied me three times" (verse 38).

Now on the shore of Galilee Jesus announces that Peter will indeed follow Him, laying down his life for Him. The apostle who always seemed to want to take charge of things would not even have control over dressing himself for his final journey—to his execution. Tradition says that the Roman emperor Nero had Peter crucified about A.D. 64.[16] Also, tradition holds that Peter requested that he be hung upside down on the cross. The dreaded execution by crucifixion had become so sacred in his mind that Peter did not feel worthy to die in the same way as his Master.

Modern readers do not understand the horror of the fate Peter awaited. The Romans used crucifixion as a psychological weapon to destroy the will to resist of all who dared to oppose them. It was a form of death intended to make the victim suffer as long as possible before dying and at the same time instill fear in the general population. If anyone crossed their Roman masters they too would face a similar fate. The victim, generally stripped naked, had to endure one degrading experience after another. The shame of crucifixion did not end with death. The Romans, except in the case of higher-class political prisoners, usually forbade the burial of the victims. The authorities wanted the bodies to hang on the cross until animals ate them or they decayed and fell off. The fact that relatives could not bury the body brought great shame to the whole family, which was part of the intended punishment. The ancients believed that the unburied dead would not be able to join the community of the other dead.[17] Those who attempted to bury a crucified person knew that they could face a similar death.

Nor could people publicly mourn a crucified victim. If they did, Roman soldiers would immediately crucify them. The Roman author Tacitus, describing a mass execution by the emperor Tiberius, said that the authorities would not permit "relatives or friends to stand near, to weep over them, or even to view them too long; but a cordon of sentries, with eyes for each beholder's sorrow, escorted the rotting carcasses, as they were dragged to the Tiber, there to float with the current or drift to the bank, with none to commit them to the flames."[18]

One can understand why the disciples fled for their lives during Jesus' crucifixion. His women followers put their lives at great risk even when they stood some distance away (Matt. 27:55). Except for John, who may have been in his early teens and thus perhaps ignored by the soldiers, most of the men, including Peter, had disappeared.

Death by execution was regarded as so shameful that early Christians rarely employed the cross as a symbol of their faith. They used a fish or other symbols. Instead of depicting Jesus on a cross, they portrayed Him as a young beardless shepherd, often carrying a lamb on His shoulders, an image the pagans also used for the god Bacchus. It would be several centuries before the cross and crucifixion scenes became common in Christian art.

Like Peter and Paul, most of the apostles would experience martyrdom. But it would not be a spur-of-the-moment thing. They witnessed to their long and deep relationship with their Saviour.

---

[1] See, for example, Eusebius, *The History of the Church From Christ to Constantine,* trans. G. A. Williams (New York: Dorset Press, 1965), pp. 334, 338. Giuseppe Ricciotti's *The Age of Martyrs: Christianity From Diocletian to Constantine,* trans. Anthony Bull (New York: Barnes and Noble, 1992), collects additional accounts from other early sources. David W. Bercot, ed., *A Dictionary of Early Christian Beliefs: A Reference Guide to More Than 700 Topics Discussed by the Early Church Fathers* (Peabody, Mass.: Hendrickson Publishers, 1998) collects early statements about martyrdom.

[2] Jewish writings presented Abel as the first martyr. See, for example, 4 Maccabees 18:10-19 in C. Keener, *IVP Bible Background Commentary: New*

Testament, p. 674.

[3] Sara Japhat, *I & II Chronicles: A Commentary* (Louisville, Ky.: Westminster/John Knox Press, 1993), p. 847.

[4] Second Chronicles puts much more emphasis on Joash's failings than does the parallel account in 2 Kings.

[5] Japhat, p. 850.

[6] Martin J. Selman, *2 Chronicles: A Commentary* (Leicester, Eng.: InterVarsity Press, 1994), p. 456.

[7] Matthew 23:35 apparently misnames Zechariah's father.

[8] Japhat, pp. 849, 850.

[9] Keener, p. 85.

[10] A view supported by the Jewish historian Josephus. See his *Antiquities of the Jews* 18.5.1, 2, 116-119.

[11] Keener, p. 85.

[12] *Ibid.*

[13] *Ibid.*

[14] *Ibid.,* p. 151.

[15] The Roman historian Tacitus depicted the emperor Nero as having the heads of his victims brought to him.

[16] Keener, p. 319.

[17] Perhaps we see an allusion to this belief in Revelation 20:13, in which the sea gives up the unburied dead.

[18] Tacitus, *The Annals,* trans. John Jackson (Cambridge, Mass.: Harvard University Press, 1956), vol. 3, p. 187. See also *Digestae* 3. 2. 11. 3 and Philo *In Flaccum* 72. The Romans disposed of their dead by cremation instead of burial. Not to cremate a body shamed the family much in the same way that failure to bury someone did the people of Palestine.

CHAPTER 11

A Cloud of Witnesses

As we saw earlier, faith in the Bible is far more than intellectual belief or assent. It is loyalty and trust in another. True faith is not what we can make ourselves believe, but our confidence that God will fulfill His promises. The power of faith is not ours but God's. Thus the life of faith is loyalty to God, obedience to Him, service for Him, and living a life of action in His behalf. Men and women of faith venture into the unknown for God—all the while trusting in the fact that He is in control of even the unknown. Everything they do for Him rests in the security of what God has already done or revealed. Faith thus boils down to trust built on experience. We have confidence in what He tells us about the future because He has already shown He keeps His word in His past deeds.

In Hebrews 11 the Bible honors as its heroes of faith those who demonstrated their loyalty to God in what they did in life, even to the point of death. William L. Lane regards the faith of those listed in this chapter as "characterized by firmness, reliability, and steadfastness. It is trust in God and in His promises (cf. Heb. 4:1-3; 6:1; 11:6, 17-19, 24). The context shows that what these attested witnesses affirm is the reliability of God, who is faithful to his promises (11:11). Committing themselves to God who is steadfast, these exemplars of faith were themselves made steadfast. This concept of faith is rooted in the OT, where faith and hope are closely allied. . . . The tension between faith and the realization of the promise of God that is developed throughout this section demonstrates that it is the nature of faith to render hope secure (verses 1, 9, 10, 13, 24-26, 39)."[1]

Although many use Hebrews 1:1 as a definition of what faith is, the passage is more a call for celebrating faith.[2] The verse also stresses that faith involves future reward.[3] Beyond that, the biblical writer lets us draw our own conclusion of what faith is by showing us snapshots of it in operation. Scripture here portrays how those who loyally followed God lived out their faith. Space permits us to examine only a few examples.

Abel

Hebrews 11:4 declares that Abel offered a more acceptable sacrifice than did his brother Cain. Commentators most often focus on the nature of Abel's offering—a blood sacrifice—as opposed to Cain's gift of "the fruit of the ground" (Gen. 4:3). But, as we have seen elsewhere, more than that is going on here. God did accept plant-based offerings (Lev. 2; 6:14-23),[4] so the difference between the two brothers involves much more than that one had an animal sacrifice and the other a plant offering. Abel's greatest sacrifice was a life of total obedience and relationship with God. He recognized not only his need for God as a Saviour but also God's role and authority in his life. Cain, however, rejected God's priority and rulership. He wanted God's protection (Gen. 4:14) but that was about all.

The core of the Old Testament concept of righteousness was having right relationships with others. Abel had a right relationship with God, but Cain had wrong relationships not only with the Lord but also with his brother and the rest of the human race. When God sent him into exile, Cain feared all other human beings. Unlike his brother Abel, he did not know how to have a right relationship with anybody.

Abel's blood sacrifice symbolized God's mercy and grace. The Lord is a deity of mercy and grace in all His dealings with His creation. Even Cain's punishment reflects God's compassion and forgiveness as He protected the fugitive's life with a mysterious mark. But Cain, like Abel, could have known even greater grace if he had shared his brother's relationship with their Creator and Redeemer.

Enoch

Belief in God involves far more than just intellectually accepting that He exists, though all faith must begin there. Some married people believe in the existence of their spouses but may have no real relationship with them. Too often they do not live as if married, having no emotional or even physical contact with their mates. Perhaps they are having affairs with others outside the marital relationship. The fact that they are married has little or no effect on their lives.

People do the same with God. For example, surveys indicate that the majority of people in North America believe in God's existence. But only a fraction of them attend church or are involved in any kind of religious activity. Even those who do go to church often restrict their religious life to church hours. Their belief is only intellectual at best and even then often superficial. It has little impact on what they do with most of their life. With them God is only a concept, a theoretical abstraction. The Lord does not permeate every aspect of daily life.

But Enoch's faith touched every part of his existence. Hebrews 11:6 declares not only that God exists[5] but also that He interacts with those who seek Him. He rewards those who reach out to Him and desire a relationship with Him. Genesis 5:24 says that Enoch "walked with God." Scripture uses the expression "walked with God" only of Enoch and Noah (Gen. 6:9). The broader image of "walking" is a biblical symbol for obedience and religious lifestyle. The apostle Paul calls for Christians to "walk" with God—to live as He commands (see, for example, Rom. 6:4; 8:4; 14:15). God filled every moment and activity of Enoch's life. The patriarch grew so close to God that the Lord decided not to allow death to break the relationship, but translated him.[6] Again, the patriarch's faith was not one of intellectual assent, but ultimate relationship and loyalty.

Abraham

For years Abraham had followed God's leading. He had left his urban and sophisticated life in Ur of Chaldees, stopped for a time in Haran, then began the tent-dwelling and wandering existence of a pastoralist in a harsh and foreign country in which he was only a tolerated outsider (Gen. 11:31, 32; 12:1-9). During this time the Lord promised him a son who would begin a great nation. But Abraham and his wife grew old, and no children of their own came. Several times the patriarch attempted to help God fulfill His promise, but the Lord kept telling him that He alone would provide a son. And He did.

Now Abraham's son was reaching what the ancient world considered adulthood. Isaac would soon marry and father children. Abraham could see the beginning of that great nation the Lord had vowed to make of him. Then God shattered everything. Devastated, Abraham listened in horror as the Lord asked him to sacrifice his special son.

The patriarch had heard God's voice too many times for him to dismiss the divine command as only a hallucination. Abraham must have struggled in his mind over God's summons to sacrifice his son. It would seemingly destroy all that God had promised, and even worse, it called into question everything Abraham had come to understand about the divine character. But "on the basis of his own rich experience with God" he "accepted what he could not understand."[7]

According to Hebrews 11:19 the patriarch concluded that God would somehow restore Isaac, perhaps through resurrection. In fact, the biblical writer considers God's halting of the sacrifice a "foreshadowing" of God's ability to raise the dead.[8] Abraham had faith because his years of relationship with God had taught him that he could trust the Lord to work things out. God had already kept His promise of a son and repeatedly demonstrated His trustworthiness. It had taken Abraham a long time to grasp that fact. But at last he had come to trust, to remain loyal to God no matter what.

Now he had to put that trust into concrete action by taking Isaac to Mount Moriah. The Lord had brought the son of promise into existence. If He now asked for Isaac back, He would fulfill the divine promise still another way. Abraham probably never understood the full implications of his statement to Isaac: "God himself will provide the lamb for a burnt offering, my son" (Gen.

22:8). But he knew God's reliability, and that is the most important thing any follower of God must learn. It's the core of any true faith.

Rahab

Matthew's genealogy of Christ lists four women, an unusual practice both in the Bible and the ancient world that primarily traced descent through the male line. Even more startling is who those women were: Tamar (Matt. 1:3), a Canaanite woman who tricked her father-in-law into sex with her; Rahab (verse 5), a Canaanite prostitute; Ruth (verse 5), a Moabite woman; and Bathsheba (verse 6), who had an adulterous affair with David (notice that Matthew deliberately reminds us of that fact by identifying her only as the wife of Uriah). None of them were the kind of people we would expect to find as the ancestors of the Messiah.

Yet Hebrews 11:31 selects Rahab as an example of great faith. Not only was she a prostitute, but she lied and betrayed her own people. How could anyone extol her as an example of the kind of faith God expects? First, she believed in the God of the Hebrews. "The Lord your God is indeed God in heaven above and on earth below," she told the two Hebrew spies (Joshua 2:11). She followed through on her belief that Israel's God had given her land to the Hebrews (verses 9, 24) by helping the spies escape from Jericho.

Rahab had more confidence in the power of the God of Abraham, Isaac, and Jacob than did many of the Israelites themselves. But even more, she committed her life and those of her family to the protection of the foreign God (verses 12, 13). "By faith Rahab the prostitute did not perish with those who were disobedient, because she had received the spies in peace" (Heb. 11:31). The verse hints at more than the fate of her fellow citizens of Jericho. "Disobedient" is the same term the book of Hebrews employs for the Hebrews who perished in the wilderness (Heb. 3:16-19). Rahab had more trust in God than did His own people.

She put her life in danger when she protected the spies. Then the fact that Joshua's men could find her in the destroyed city (Joshua 6:22, 23) meant that she had put the scarlet cord (Joshua

2:18) in the window. The act concretely demonstrated her faith. After the destruction of Jericho she became a part of God's people (Joshua 6:25). As with all the spiritual heroes of Hebrews 11, her faith was not just mental assent, but trust put into action—action that was risky. Yet she staked her existence and that of her family on it. Hers was faith lived, not just believed. And it was faith in God's dealings with His people and those who joined them.

The Promise Yet Awaits

If you examine those named in Hebrews 11 you will find that (except for Enoch) Scripture reveals that all of them had flaws and failures. The ones we have already looked at had their imperfections. In addition, Gideon made an object termed an ephod that became an idol to Israel (Judges 8:22-27). Barak struggled with doubt (Judges 4:6-9). David's life was one of constant violence and repeated mistakes, and Samuel's sons disgraced him (1 Sam. 8:3). The prophets had their human weaknesses.

God's heroes of faith were not perfect beings. But when crises came, they showed their faith by trusting God and putting their faith into action. As we have already pointed out, that is the beginning and core of true biblical faith. But faith involves still more than this.

Some of God's heroes were successful in this life, delivering His people from an oppressor or presenting a message in His name. But even they did not receive all that God promised. Others met with what seemed total failure (Heb. 11:35-38). What God promised them they still await. He will give it to them in the next life only, after the resurrection. But despite the apparent failure they still clung to their belief that God would keep His word. And they demonstrated that faith by a willingness to do for God whatever He requested.

Perhaps we feel that we receive no reward in this life. Neither did many of those in Hebrews 11. Reward will come when Christ returns—but only to those who begin lives of trust, loyalty, and obedience now.

Hebrews 11 began with the idea that "faith is the assurance

of things hoped for, the conviction of things not seen" (verse 1). Such a concept would have shocked the Greek intellectuals of New Testament times, because they regarded faith "as a state of mind characteristic of the uneducated, who believe something on hearsay without being able to give precise reasons for their belief." [9] True, the men and women of Hebrews might not be able to offer philosophical arguments in defense of their trust in God, but from personal experience and from the biblical revelation of what He had done in the past, they knew that He would honor His promises in the future—promises He would bring to pass in even better ways (verse 40). If we follow their example, we will have nothing to fear in our own lives and futures.

---

[1] William L. Lane, *Hebrews 9-13*, Word Biblical Commentary (Dallas: Word Books, 1991), vol. 47b, pp. 315, 316.

[2] *Ibid.*, p. 328.

[3] C. Keener, *IVP Bible Background Commentary: New Testament*, p. 673.

[4] "The *offering* is a *minḥâ*, which in human affairs was a gift of homage or allegiance and, as a ritual term, could describe either animal or more often cereal offerings (eg. 1 Sam. 2:17; Lev. 2:1). . . . The New Testament draws out the further important implications that Cain's life, unlike Abel's, gave the lie to his offering (1 John 3:12) and that Abel's faith was decisive for his acceptance (Heb. 11:4)" (D. Kidner, *Genesis*, p. 75).

[5] In biblical times belief in God also led to a nonbelief in other gods. During Judaism's struggle with Greek culture the Jews proclaimed, "We worship only the God who exists" (4 Maccabees 5:24).

[6] For additional evidence of the understanding that Enoch did not die, see Lane, p. 336. Enoch is seventh in line in the genealogy in Genesis 5. Interestingly, the seventh person in the Mesopotamian list of preflood rulers, Utuabzu, ascended to heaven (J. Walton and V. Matthews, *IVP Bible Background Commentary: Genesis-Deuteronomy*, p. 25).

[7] W. Lane, p.360.

[8] *Ibid.*, p. 362.

[9] *Ibid.*, p. 316.

CHAPTER 12

Women in a Male World

The biblical world was much more divided along gender lines than the modern Western world. As we noted in the chapter on Joseph, women were responsible for life in the home and men generally had charge of life outside it. But that did not mean that women were inferior or less important or that they were always restricted to the home. Life was hard, and both sexes had to work as a team to survive. They labored together in the fields, among the flocks, and around the home. The human race would long ago have perished if women did nothing more than raise children and keep house.

For example, today we may at first think of technology as a male domain. But in biblical times women had control of most technical processes that did not require brute physical force.[1] They dyed and wove fabrics, prepared and cooked food, operated home industries, took care of daily medical needs, and performed countless other tasks now often relegated to specialists, frequently men. The modern world does not view such processes as technology unless done in a factory, but they are complex and require technical knowledge and skill. In the ancient world men did not go off to an industrial plant or office to earn a living for their families and then bring it home to their wives. Life was a cooperative venture for both sexes. God had intended it that way.

He made human beings to be His stewards of creation, His representatives on earth. Scripture says He created them in His image, and that it takes both male and female together to fully reflect that image (Gen. 1:27). Egyptians and others set up images to stand for the rulership and authority of a king in a distant part of his realm. Men and women are God's image on earth.[2] The

Lord wants us to be His stewards and representatives in our world. It takes both genders to do His work on earth, and even in a male-dominated Bible God called women to many different tasks for Him.

Deborah—Judge of Israel

As a judge in Israel (Judges 4:4), Deborah combined the roles of national leader, prophet, legal expert, arbiter, and if need be, military leader and national deliverer.[3] But most of the time her work focused on her legal responsibilities.[4] The Israelites valued her wisdom and would bring their problems to the court she conducted under a palm tree in the hill country (verse 5). Interestingly, Scripture seems to find nothing unusual in a woman filling such a prominent public role, even though biblical society was generally patriarchal outside the home. Nor was she the only example. God also spoke through Miriam and Huldah and saved His people through Esther (see chapter 4). Obviously Deborah had to be a strong personality. (The Hebrew phrase usually translated "wife of Lappidoth" in verse 4 can also be rendered "fiery woman" or "spirited woman."[5]

The forces of King Jabin had been oppressing Israel for 20 years (verse 3). The people turned to God in repentance and sought His help. The Lord tells Deborah to commission Barak to fight Sisera, Jabin's general (verses 6, 7). To her previous forensic duties she adds a prophetic role.[6] Deborah speaks for God, summoning Israel to war. Her act parallels Samuel's appointment of Saul to battle the Amalekites (1 Sam. 15).[7] Barak is clearly inferior to her.[8] He also hesitates to accept the military leadership. "If you will go with me, I will go; but if you will not go with me, I will not go," he responds (Judges 4:8). She promises to accompany him, but warns him that "the road on which you are going will not lead to your glory, for the Lord will sell Sisera into the hand of a woman" (verse 9).

At the battle she tells him, "Up! For this is the day on which the Lord has given Sisera into your hand. The Lord is indeed going out before you" (verse 14). The description of the battle has many echoes of the Exodus.[9] Deborah orders Barak to advance (verse 14; cf. Ex. 14:15). The enemy chariot force panics (Judges 4:15; cf. Ex. 14:24, 25), a flash flood in the brook Kishon sweeps them away (Judges 5:21; cf. Ex. 14:26-28), and afterward Deborah sings a song of victory (Judges 5; cf. Ex. 15). Although Judges 5:1 lists both her and Barak as giving the song, the feminine verb suggests she was the prime singer, with Barak joining in later. Exodus 15 begins with Moses singing, then in verse 20 switches to Miriam. Thus the narrator compares Deborah to both Moses and Miriam.

God worked through both Deborah and Barak to deliver Israel. Both men and women are to be His channels of salvation. Joining Deborah in freeing Israel was another woman, Jael (Judges 4:17-22; 5:24-27). Interestingly, she was not an Israelite but a member of the Kenite tribe, a nomadic clan allied with Israel. Scripture speaks of a number of women who associated themselves with God's people. The most famous is that of the Moabite Ruth.

"Your People Shall Be My People"

In our individualistic Western world we do not realize what a difficult and even amazing decision Ruth made when she chose to follow Naomi back to Bethlehem and worship her God.

Both women were widows. A widow in the biblical world was a woman without male relatives to help support her. Apart from prostitution, there was no way for a single woman without family to survive. A widow had to find another husband, return to her father's household, be accepted into some other household, or depend on the charity of the larger community. When Naomi learned that God had provided His people in Judah with food once again, she decided to return to her home in Bethlehem (Ruth 1:7).

The two daughters-in-law accompanied her for a ways. Katharine Doob Sakenfeld notes that the wording of verse 7 hints that all three women were prepared to journey to Bethlehem. Sakenfeld suggests that Naomi had second thoughts about the two younger women going with her.[10] Perhaps Naomi does not want them around to remind her of the cruel blow life has dealt her. Or she does not want to be responsible for two unmarried foreign women. Whatever the reason, she is bitter and puts the blame for all that has happened squarely on God (verses 13, 20, 21). When she reaches Bethlehem she at first does not even acknowledge Ruth's presence with her (Naomi declares that she came back "empty" [verse 21]), and does not talk to her daughter-in-law until Ruth initiates the conversation (cf. Ruth 2:2).

On the road to Bethlehem Naomi tells Ruth and her sister-in-law to return to their mothers' households (Ruth 1:8). "May the Lord deal kindly with you, as you have dealt with the dead and with me" (verse 9). The expression "deal kindly" incorporates the Hebrew word *ḥesed*, variously translated as "kindness," "faithfulness," or "loyalty." *Ḥesed* is the theme of the entire book. But here Naomi uses *ḥesed* in a slightly different way. "The words [of verse 9] may reflect not just a general wish, but a formulaic expression by which to bring a relationship to an end without recrimination or sense of disloyalty on either side. By invoking divine *ḥesed* on behalf of Ruth and Orpah, Naomi signals to them that they are free of any continuing commitment to her."[11]

Returning home was the only sensible thing for the two younger widows to do. There among their own families they would find material and emotional support and perhaps new husbands. For a time both daughters-in-law persist in wanting to accompany her, then Orpah submits to common sense and heads back to her family. Despite the generations of commentators who have criticized her and treated her almost as an apostate, she was only doing what her mother-in-law urged her to do. Naomi's willingness "to bring the relationship to a close both preempt a negative interpretation of Orpah's choice and set the stage for revealing the depth of Ruth's loyalty (*ḥesed*, cf. 3:10) in her decision to accompany Naomi."[12] As readers we can see that Orpah passed up the opportunity to join God's people, but the book's author is not faulting her for returning to her family.

Three times Naomi advised Ruth not to accompany her to

Bethlehem. Asian and Christian cultures hold Ruth up as a role model of how a dutiful daughter-in-law should obey every word of her mother-in-law. But they do not read Scripture carefully—they project into it their cultural bias. Ruth actually disobeyed Naomi here.

Ruth does not want to return to her family. She has found something in Naomi that makes her "cling" to her (Ruth 1:14), the same word used in Genesis 2:24 in which a man leaves his mother and "clings" to his wife. Because of what she has seen in Naomi's character and the God she represents, Ruth chooses the highly dangerous option of remaining with Naomi. She will stay with her mother-in-law both in life and in death (verse 17), and Scripture honors her for it.

In the ancient world one rarely changed gods. Religious conversions as we understand them were almost unknown. "Religion was bound up with ethnicity in biblical times; each people had its land and its gods (cf. Micah 4:5), so that to change religion meant to change nationality."[13] Even those who might move to another country usually kept their religion because it was a part of their national identity,[14] and were thus always considered foreigners. As we noticed in the chapter on Judas the word translated "Jew" really meant a national designation. No matter where a Jew lived people always considered him or her a Judean. Even today many cultures equate national identity with a specific religion. To be a Serb is to be an Orthodox Christian, Croatians are Catholic, and the true citizens of Islamic countries are Muslim.

But Ruth had seen in her life with Naomi a God that attracted her. She was willing to turn her back on everything she had known—her home, her people, her nationality, and her religion—to be with Naomi and worship her mother-in-law's God (verses 16, 17). In Bethlehem she would bring security and happiness to Naomi. Naomi committed her daughters-in-law to the loving-kindness (*ḥesed*) of God, and God would show that *ḥesed* to Naomi through Ruth. And Ruth would become the ancestor of Jesus (Matt. 1:5), who would manifest *ḥesed* to the whole world.

"The Lord Is With You"

Families in the biblical world arranged betrothals when daughters were quite young, usually still girls. The general pattern was for the betrothal to take place when the girl was 13, and the marriage would be consummated about a year later.[15] If the girl's fiancé died, biblical culture considered her a widow.[16] The groom paid at least half the bride price at the time of betrothal. A betrothal was as legal and binding as marriage itself and required divorce proceedings to terminate. Biblical law considered sexual intercourse between a betrothed woman and another man as adultery (Deut. 22:23, 24). The only difference between betrothal and marriage was that the couple did not live together.

Mary, the future mother of Jesus, was probably only in her early teens when the angel Gabriel came to tell her that she would give birth to Christ. Gabriel's announcement reflects both Old Testament birth annunciations and Old Testament divine call narratives. God called Mary to the office of being Jesus' human mother.[17] The announcement must have been overwhelming to the girl. Unlike Zechariah (Luke 1:18-20), she did believe Gabriel even though his message "perplexed" her (verse 29; cf. verse 34). But she suddenly had to cope with something that on one hand was an awesome honor and responsibility, yet on the other hand would bring great shame and criticism to her and those around her.

Although Scripture does not depict the gossip and criticism that she must have endured, it does show how her husband Joseph reacted. He, "being a righteous man and unwilling to expose her to public disgrace, planned to dismiss her quietly" (Matt. 1:19). The Old Testament specified death as the punishment for a betrothed woman caught in adultery. Even if New Testament society rarely if ever followed the biblical law here, a pregnant betrothed girl would have had a hard time finding another husband if the man she was currently betrothed to should divorce her.

Jesus had to frequently deal with hints of His questionable birth (John 8:41; 9:29). In the small village of Nazareth with its lack of privacy, gossip and rumor would have rapidly spread word of Mary's pregnancy. But she was willing to endure the stigma. "Here am I, the servant of the Lord," she told Gabriel. "Let it be with me according to your word" (Luke 1:38). The word here for "handmaid" or "servant" means "slave girl" and signifies complete obedience.[18] Mary thus employs the regular Old Testament symbol for submission and acquiescence (see, for example, 1 Sam. 1:18; 25:41; 2 Sam. 9:6, 11; 2 Kings 4:2).[19] A little later she declares, "My soul magnifies the Lord, and my spirit rejoices in God my Savior, for he has looked with favor on the lowliness of his servant. Surely, from now on all generations will call me blessed; for the Mighty One has done great things for me, and holy is his name" (verses 47-49).[20]

God chose Mary to bear Jesus and be His human mother because even in her short life she had already demonstrated her character and allegiance to God. Throughout the annunciation and infancy stories Luke portrays her as deeply thoughtful (Luke 1:29; 2:19, 51), obedient (Luke 1:38), believing (verse 45), worshipful (verse 46), and devoted to biblical law and piety (Luke 2:22-51). She accepted God's will and left the problems for Him to resolve.

A Forgiven Woman

New Testament culture considered it virtuous to invite a teacher for dinner, particularly if he were from out of town or had just taught at the synagogue.[21] In Luke 7:36-50 a Pharisee named Simon seeks to honor Jesus by asking Him to a formal dinner. The custom at banquets was to recline on cushions lining three sides of a square. The fourth side would be open for the servants to bring food to the low table. The guests would face the table, with their feet extending away from it. Jesus would have His left arm on the table and His feet pointing back toward the wall behind Him. Because of the physical arrangement of the diners and the fact that the room would have no large windows and would be only dimly lit, no one would have noticed a woman approaching Jesus from behind.

In the upper levels of society women did not eat with men on formal occasions. They retired to their own quarters. Only among the rural peasants did men and women regularly dine together. Society expected men to eat and discuss important political and philosophical topics while the women gossiped among themselves about children and weddings. So it surprised the men to suddenly smell an opened box of perfume and to look up and see a nonservant woman in the room.

Even more startling was the fact that she was weeping and bathing Jesus' feet with her tears. John Nolland regards her tears as ones of remorse, not anguish. Since she had found peace in Jesus, the sorrow of regret was "suffused with the warmth of grateful affection."[22] Then to compound the men's shock the woman began drying Jesus' feet with her hair (Luke 7:38). Religious adult women kept their hair covered. At least in cities, only prostitutes went about with their hair uncovered and falling over their shoulders and back. For the woman at the banquet to dry Jesus' feet with her unbound hair immediately labeled her as promiscuous. Perfume was also a trademark of prostitution.

The parallel account in Mark 14:3-5 calls the ointment nard[23] and says it was worth 300 denarii, an amount a laborer would have to work for six months to earn. The ointment was in an alabaster jar or vessel that probably had been imported from as far away as Nepal.[24] In the ancient world the spice and perfume trade was economically equivalent to what the petroleum industry has been in the past century. Because people did not bathe regularly, the streets were full of raw sewage, and the taste of spoiled food needed masking, incenses, perfumes, and spices were in great demand, especially among the wealthy. Merchants shipped them over trade routes hundreds and even thousands of miles long. People made and spent fortunes on them. Roman emperors would burn incense worth hundreds of thousands of dollars at banquets just to flaunt their wealth.

The woman, described as a sinner, had probably earned the money to buy the valuable perfume by working as a prostitute. Since the ancient world did not have interest-bearing savings accounts, certificates of deposit, or stocks and bonds to invest in, many bought perfumes and spices as a means of safely storing their wealth in a way that would at the same time continue to increase in value. When she broke the expensive alabaster jar or box and poured its contents on Jesus, she was—in the eyes of those present—squandering a small fortune (Mark 14:4, 5).

Even more scandalous, the woman kissed Jesus' feet.

The fact that Jesus continued to permit the woman to anoint and wash His feet greatly disturbed His host, Simon. If Jesus were truly a prophet, he reasoned to himself, the Master had to know what kind of woman she was. Surely He would have stopped her (Luke 7:39). But to Simon's surprise, Jesus knew what was going on in Simon's mind. The Master told Simon a parable about forgiveness (verses 41, 42). The Pharisee immediately grasped Jesus' moral that greater forgiveness elicits greater love (verse 43).

Then, turning to the woman, Jesus reminded His host that he had not provided the customary foot washing before the meal (verse 44). Since the streets were clogged with human and animal waste, a good host had the servants wash the guests' feet during the first course of the meal and perhaps apply perfume. But though Simon overlooked it, the woman had bathed and dried His feet. People in Middle Eastern cultures greeted each other with a kiss (verse 45; cf. Rom. 16:16; 1 Cor. 16:20; 1 Peter 5:14). Simon had neglected that, but not the woman who had kissed Jesus' feet. Thoughtful hosts would anoint a guest's head with common olive oil—but not Simon (verse 46). Yet the woman used expensive perfume.

Yes, the woman was a sinner. But she had been forgiven much and responded with appropriate love (verse 47). Then to reinforce His point, Jesus told her, "Your sins are forgiven" (verse 48). His act of forgiveness stirred up great discussion. The fact that only God can forgive sins lay behind the other guests' question to each other, "Who is this who even forgives sins?" (verse 49). As He did many times throughout the Gospels Jesus was claiming a divine prerogative. Finally He commented to the woman, "Your faith has saved you" (verse 50). Her faith was relationship and loyalty to Him. His statement showed that the love He said she had displayed "was the consequence, not the cause, of her salvation." [25]

The woman may have been a sinner and outcast in the eyes of the male dinner guests. But Jesus understood the motivation behind everything she did.

---

[1] L. Perdue, J. Blenkinsopp, J. Collins, and C. Meyers, *Families in Ancient Israel*, p. 26.

[2] *Anchor Bible Dictionary*, vol. 3, p. 389.

[3] Victor H. Matthews goes so far as to see the judges as more military leaders than judicial or religious leaders, since the book of Judges most often depicts them as conducting God-directed campaigns against national enemies (Victor H. Matthews, *Manners and Customs in the Bible: An Illustrated Guide to Daily Life in Bible Times* [Peabody, Mass.: Hendrickson Publishers, 1986], p. 70).

[4] Alberto Soggin, *Judges: A Commentary* (Philadelphia: Westminster Press, 1981), pp. 64, 71, 72.

[5] *Harper's Bible Commentary*, p. 250.

[6] Soggin, pp. 71, 72.

[7] *Harper's Bible Commentary*, p. 250.

[8] Soggin, p. 71.

[9] *Ibid.*, p. 76.

[10] Sakenfeld, Ruth, p. 23.

[11] *Ibid.*, p. 24.

[12] *Ibid.*

[13] *Harper's Bible Commentary*, p. 263.

[14] That does not mean that they might not be tempted to worship additional gods, especially, as we saw when we considered Naaman's servant girl, when the gods of the new country appeared to have defeated the God of Israel. The exiles in Babylon struggled with this question when they asked, "How could we sing the Lord's song in a foreign land?" (Ps. 137:4). Still, only drastic circumstances could lead a person to change religion in the modern sense.

[15] Nolland, *Luke 1-9:20*, p. 58.

[16] C. Keener, *IVP Bible Background Commentary: New Testament*, p. 47.

[17] *Ibid.*, p. 190.

[18] L. Morris, *Luke*, p. 82.

[19] Keener, p. 190.

[20] Note that Mary's speech, often called the "Magnificat," is in poetry. Poetry was the idiom of important topics. Men would use formal poetry, while women composed extemporaneous poetry, as is the case here (Malina and Rhorbaugh, *Synoptic Gospels*, pp. 293, 294). Mary's poem echoes that of Hannah in 1 Samuel 2:1-10.

[21] Keener, p. 208.

[22] Nolland, p. 354.

[23] Mark has the woman pouring the nard over Jesus' head. Ointment soothed the dry skin of the scalp. A good host would provide it for guests.

[24] *Anchor Bible Dictionary*, vol. 5, p. 227.

[25] Morris, p. 163.

CHAPTER 13

Little Acts, Big Consequences

Those who live in the modern West with its strong sense of individualism have lost much of their sense of community. They have largely forgotten how human beings are inextricably bound to each other in a web of relationships, and how they need each other. As a result, they pay a terrible price in loneliness. Also, they have a hard time understanding many Bible stories that reflect the group identity that has persisted throughout most of human history and still dominates society in much of the world. But even in cultures that stress individualism we find that lives intertwine with each other. What a person does affects those around him or her. This was especially so in Bible times.

Lot and His Wife

Bible commentators understandably condemn Lot's wife for clinging to her life in Sodom, but Lot himself must share much of the blame for her behavior. He had made the decision to dwell in the morally and spiritually dangerous city of Sodom (Gen. 13:11, 12). The city had a powerful influence on him and his family. When the angels came to warn them of the city's impending doom, he "lingered" (Gen. 19:16). The angels had to drag him, his wife, and two of his daughters away by the hand. The biblical account regards such forceful action as "the Lord being merciful to him." Once outside the city, the angels urged, "Flee for your life; do not look back or stop anywhere in the Plain; flee to the hills, or else you will be consumed" (verse 17).

But Lot protested, "Oh, no, my lords, your servant has found favor with you, and you have shown me great kindness in saving my life; but I cannot flee to the hills, for fear the disaster will overtake me and I die" (verses 18, 19). Lot either did not trust that God would save him—even after all the miraculous evidence of God's protection that he had already experienced—or he was seeking an excuse to stay in the area. Pointing to a nearby town, he bargained with the angels. "Look, that city is near enough to flee to, and it is a little one." By implication he meant that it was not as evil simply through not being as big as Sodom and not as deserving of destruction. "Let me escape there—is it not a little one?—and my life will be saved!" (verse 20).

The angels granted his audacious request, promising that nothing will harm Zoar (the name means "little") (verse 21). The spokesangel explained that he could not destroy Sodom until Lot reached safety (verse 22). Lot should have known that if God had sent His angels to rescue him, He would do everything possible to protect him. The man's worries about his safety were, if nothing else, implied doubts about God's power and intention. Derek Kidner comments that we can all see ourselves as potential Lots, "lingering, quibbling . . . wheedling a last concession as he is dragged to safety. Not even brimstone will make a pilgrim of him: he must have his little Sodom again if life is to be supportable (20c)."[1]

His continual reluctance had its effect on his wife. She may have valued her former home more than God's command to flee, but she did only what her husband had already been demonstrating throughout much of his life. He might not have physically glanced back as she did, but his mind was still staring over his shoulder at Sodom.

Unholy Fire

Certain actions can be more dangerous in some situations than others. A parent may tell a child racing around in a playground simply to be careful. But if the youngster does the same thing on a busy street, the mother or father will scream, dash after the child, and spank him or her for disobedience. The difference is where or in what situation the deed takes place. Behavior that people will overlook during normal times may have to be dealt with severely during periods of crisis. The story of Nadab and Abihu provides one biblical example of such.

Many of the incidents in which God seems to react harshly occur during times of great danger to His people, either physical or spiritual. To understand fully the significance of what the two priests did, we must look at it in its full historical context. As soon as God revealed to Moses the plan for constructing the tabernacle (Ex. 25-31), the Israelites cast the golden calf (Ex. 32:10), but Moses pleaded for them (verses 11-13),[2] and the Lord "changed his mind" (verse 14). Moses himself purged some of the disruptive elements (verses 21-29). Then in Leviticus 8 and 9 the tabernacle is consecrated, only to have the two priests offer "unholy fire" (Lev. 10:1). God destroys them with His own fire (verse 2). In each incident someone does something during a period in which the identity and existence of the community of faith are under threat.

The Hebrew word used to describe the "strange" (KJV) or "unholy" fire is a term that refers to something or somebody that is where it should not be (see Ex. 29:33; 30:33; Isa. 1:7).[3] The fire was out of place because it violated all the characteristics for proper sacrificial ritual that God had given Moses.[4]

1. The priests took their own censers—flat pans or shovel-like tools for carrying burning coals—and burned incense in them. The coals should have come from the altar of burnt offering (cf. Lev. 16:12). Since the biblical account does not mention their obtaining live coals from the altar, the two sons of Aaron must have gotten them from another source.

2. The biblical regulations for sacrifice mention only the high priest ever placing incense on a censer or coals and presenting it to God. Even he did it only on the Day of Atonement. Nadab and Abihu were usurping the role of high priest. Harrison suggests that they were motivated by pride, ambition, jealousy, or impatience.[5] Any of these would have violated God's plan for the priesthood: "Through those who are near me I will show myself holy, and before all the people I will be glorified" (Lev. 10:3). Abihu and Nadab had had the privilege, along with Moses,

Aaron, and the 70 elders, of seeing a manifestation of God Himself (Ex. 24:1, 9, 10). Unfortunately, they had not gained a sense of awe. They misrepresented God's character and chose to do things their own way.

3. Clearly neither priest had consulted with Moses or their father, Aaron, about the change in procedure. Their impious act could have been the result of either disobedience toward human authority or defiance toward God Himself. Or it may have been in imitation of Egyptian practice.

4. Sprinkling coals on incense instead of following biblical regulations could have been interpreted as offering incense to pagan deities (cf. Jer. 44:25).

In addition, the incense might not have been properly mixed according to divine instruction (Ex. 30:34-38); the men might have used their own censers instead of ones specifically prepared for cultic use; or, in light of Leviticus 10:9, the priests might have been drunk. Both the Bible (Isa. 28:7) and ancient Near Eastern documents hint at pagan ritualistic intoxication.[6] In a culture that carefully followed religious ritual and procedure, any of these would have been a deliberate rejection of divine instruction.

The priesthood was to represent God's character to His people. Sadly, though, Nadab and Abihu behaved like the priests they had known in Egypt. There, religious ritual was magic to control the gods, not to depict divine nature. But even Egyptian priests would have been more careful in following proper ritual practice. Egyptian priests served the gods, but society did not care much how they lived off duty. For Israel, though, "holiness was an ethical attribute of the divine character which had to be reflected in their own lives and behaviour, since they were bound by covenant to the God of Sinai."[7]

The nation of Israel had already faced a series of crises that had rocked it to the core. If God now overlooked the priest's behavior, the whole Hebrew community could fall apart. Harrison comments that "it appears difficult to believe that the offense committed was purely accidental in nature. The reversal of values whereby what is unholy is offered to the Lord as though it were something sacred and consecrated is diametrically opposed to all for which the Sinai covenant stood."[8] Nadab and Abihu were deliberately racing in spiritual traffic. God had to punish them to protect the rest of His people from following their example.

Blindness Leads to Spiritual Sight

Sometimes those with the greatest potential turn themselves into the greatest disasters. The "angel of the Lord," who in Bible incidents is usually if not always God incarnate, came to the wife of a man of the tribe of Dan named Manoah. The Being announced that she would give birth to a son "who shall begin to deliver Israel from the hand of the Philistines" (Judges 13:5). But how or even whether prophecy can be fulfilled can be conditional upon human response.

Samson's life began with great promise. But through a series of bad decisions—little decisions with drastic consequences—he wound up the blind captive of the Philistines. Soon they began advancing into the hill country where the tribes of Israel lived. Although Samson used his supernatural strength to fight the invaders, he did not learn a crucial lesson God had been trying to teach him.

One time the Spirit of God had enabled him to kill 1,000 Philistines with the jawbone of an ass (Judges 15:14-17). Immediately afterward he succumbed to extreme thirst and prayed to God for help (verse 18). "His response not only reveals his dependence on God; it also makes a crucial theological point: the strong man cannot save himself. God provides Samson with water, and another place receives its name, En-hakkore, 'the spring of the caller' (15:18-19)."[9] Unfortunately, Samson soon forgot the divine lesson. He came to depend on his own strength, on his gift from God instead of the Giver of that gift. And he indulged in compromising relationships.

Although Samson prided himself on his ability to trick his enemies, eventually they outwitted him, and he became their slave. He played silly and petty riddles with Delilah and paid a terrible price for his foolishness. But God did not give up on him.

To enable Samson to see spiritually, God had to allow him to become blind physically.

The Philistines assigned him to grinding flour. Modern readers visualize him pushing a massive millstone around and around. But it is highly likely that he used a saddle quern. Day after day, in a kneeling position, he would have rubbed a small upper stone back and forth across a larger lower stone. Grinding flour in the ancient world was women's work. It was hard physical labor, and ancient skeletal remains reveal the wear and damage it did to bones and muscles. Samson's enemies sought to humiliate his masculinity by condemning him to a woman's task. But it gave him plenty of time to think about his life. He asked God to strengthen him to avenge the loss of his eyes (Judges 16:28). Although he lived in a world of physical darkness, God illuminated his mind and heart as never before.

One day his captors held a feast to honor their god Dagon, whom they believed had defeated Samson and delivered him into their hands (verse 23). As the wine flowed they decided to amuse themselves by bringing Samson from prison to perform for them. They made him stand between the central pillars that supported the roof of the local Philistine temple, now crowded with spectators (verse 25). He prayed to God, whom he once again realized was the only source of his strength, both physical and spiritual (verse 28).

When he had managed to dislodge the pillars, the collapse of the temple killed more Philistines than during all the years before (verse 30). (His death was technically not a suicide since God had granted his prayer for death.) Samson's death at last completed the divine prophecy of him as one who would begin Israel's deliverance. But God would have preferred that he had fulfilled it according to His leading.

Uzzah and the Ark

An old saying in English declares that "familiarity breeds contempt"; that is, we may lose respect for something that we have known too long. It has become such an ordinary part of our life that we cease to pay attention to it or take it seriously. Because it is always there we begin to treat it casually or even with indifference. We no longer have a sense of awe toward it. Here is a key to why Uzzah touched the sacred ark of the covenant and also why God had to deal with him in so dramatic a fashion. Also, as we shall see, Uzzah was not the only one at fault. God directed His punishment at King David as much as He did at Uzzah.

Many years before, the Philistines had captured the ark when the army of Israel had attempted to use it as a magical talisman to ensure them victory (1 Sam. 4). God inflicted plagues on the invaders, and they decided to return the ark (1 Sam. 5, 6). They put it on a cart pulled by two cows, which brought it to the field of Joshua of Beth-shemish (1 Sam. 6:12-14). Unfortunately, some of the inhabitants of Beth-shemesh let their curiosity get the better of them, and they decided to open the ark to see what was inside. To shock them into an awareness of its sacredness and that they must not treat anything connected with Him as the pagans would the cultic objects of their gods, God struck 70 of them dead (verse 19). Now suddenly afraid of the ark, the citizens of Beth-shemesh sent messengers to the people of Kiriath-jearim, asking them to take responsibility for the object. The latter village brought it to the house of Abinadab and consecrated his son Eleazar so he could be in charge of it (1 Sam. 6:20-7:1). There the ark remained until David decided to bring it to Jerusalem (1 Chron. 13:5).

Uzzah, described as a son of Abinadad (2 Sam. 6:3), had grown up in the ark's presence. It had been a constant part of his daily life. Because of that, he had lost his sense of the mystery and sacredness it represented. The ark was not magical, as the Israelite soldiers had assumed, but it was a symbol of the awesome God of the universe. When the Lord had ordered the ark's construction, He had stipulated that it be covered and transported by priests on special carrying poles. Nor must anyone touch it (Num. 4:5-15). But now they had put it on a new cart (2 Sam. 6:3), perhaps uncovered and in imitation of what the Philistines had done when they returned it to the Israelites (1 Sam. 6:7). But what God let the pagan Philistines do, He could not permit Israel to do. The oxen caused the ark to shift on the wagon, and Uzzah instinctively reached out to steady it (2 Sam. 6:6) as he would any other unstable load. That was the problem. It should not have been on a wagon in the first place, but since it was, God would protect it. Uzzah's instant death emphasized the point.

Uzzah had taken the sacred for granted. But he was not alone—or really the worst offender. The command to transport the ark had come from David. Part of his motivation must have been a desire to strengthen his political position by having the ark's authoritative presence in his new seat of power, Jerusalem. The king wanted to use the ancient symbol of the ark to legitimize his rule. "While this move may have been an act of good faith, it is also a nervy act of calculation."[10] Uzzah's death made David both angry and afraid (verses 8, 9). He lost face when the man died while on the king's mission, and at the same time he realized that God was not his tool or automatic supporter. He too had begun to take God for granted.

David, "who had experienced wonderful protection over the years from the Lord his God, and had known unusual intimacy with him, had to come to terms with the fact that he had overstepped the mark, and presumed upon the relationship, by failing to observe the regulations laid down to safeguard respect for God's holiness."[11] When he finally did take the ark to Jerusalem, the priests made sure that they moved it by its carrying poles (verse 13).

God cannot allow anyone to presume upon Him, take Him for granted, or manipulate Him for human advantage. Humanity must never attempt to control God. He alone is to be sovereign.

The Greedy Servant

After God healed Naaman's leprosy in the muddy Jordan River, the Syrian officer returned to Elisha and announced, "Now I know that there is no God in all the earth except in Israel; please accept a present from your servant" (2 Kings 5:15). But the prophet replied, "As the Lord lives, whom I serve, I will accept nothing!" (verse 16). Even though Naaman insisted, Elisha refused. He would not take gifts like pagan prophets. "Reward is inappropriate for one who is God's servants."[12]

But Naaman was more than just thankful for his healing. He was a convert to the God of Israel. The Syrian general requested two mule-loads of Israelite soil for the base of an altar to sacrifice to Yahweh. In addition, Naaman asked in advance for forgiveness when he had to accompany his king, as the Syrian ruler worshiped Rimmon, his national god (verses 17, 18). The healing and the encounter with Elisha had transformed Naaman. When he had first arrived he had been arrogant and hostile to the prophet (verses 11, 12). Now he was respectful and diffident,[13] calling himself "your servant" (verse 15). Elisha told him, "Go in peace" (verse 19), an acknowledgment that the Syrian was in covenant relationship with Elisha and his God.[14] Naaman showed great faith, as Jesus later testified (Luke 4:27).

The Syrian convert had gone only a short distance when Elisha's servant, Gehazi, said to himself, "My master has let that Aramean Naaman off too lightly by not accepting from him what he offered. As the Lord lives, I will run after him and get something out of him" (verse 20). The servant revealed ethnic arrogance ("that Aramean"). God had demonstrated His universal acceptance of all people. Gehazi now threatened that by his sense of exclusiveness. Nelson observes that "it is the natural reaction of religion to be exclusive rather than inclusive. As told by Luke, the reaction [by Judea's religious leaders] to Jesus' statement [about Naaman] was anger. Although Naaman lost his egocentricity (verse 11) and his ethnocentricity (verse 17) in his Jordan bath, these things still cling to Gehazi (verse 20) even before his leprosy did [later]. The story of Naaman, like those about Ruth and Jonah, fights against the tendency towards exclusiveness which infects God's people in the form of racism or nationalism (cf. Matt. 8:5-13; Acts 10:1-11:18)."[15]

Gehazi was also greedy. He swore by God that he would make Naaman pay for his healing. When the Syrian spotted him chasing along behind, trying to catch up, he jumped from his chariot and asked, "Is everything all right?" (2 Kings 5:21). The phrase *ha shalom* (literally, "the peace") often indicated the reopening of negotiations (2 Kings 9:17-19).[16] Apparently the general assumed that Elisha had changed his mind and sent his servant to bargain for a gift. Gehazi then lied that his master had asked him to request a talent[17] and two changes of clothing for two prophets who supposedly had just arrived (verse 23). People in biblical times normally owned only one or two changes of clothing at a time. Since it was handmade, clothing was much more expensive than now. Naaman granted the request, even doubling the gift of silver, and sent two servants with Gehazi to carry the heavy ingots of silver.

When Gehazi went to Elisha, the prophet inquired where his servant had been (verse 25). Gehazi claimed he hadn't gone anywhere. Elisha then revealed that he knew what his servant had done. He asked Gehazi if it was a time to enrich himself (verse 26). As punishment for his duplicity, the servant and his descendants receive Naaman's leprosy (verse 27). Gehazi's deception had reduced Elisha to just another healer for hire and undermined his credibility and influence.

The miracle had given the Syrian faith in the God of Israel, but Gehazi's greed threatened Naaman's conversion and understanding of the true God. A foreigner had been healed in body and spirit while Gehazi, a member of God's people, had let the sin of greed infect his spirit. Now God revealed the servant's spiritual disease through the physical condition of leprosy. Leprosy excluded him from the community of faith (verse 27). Another "little" sin required drastic action to prevent worse consequences.

Ananias and Sapphira

We see the same principle at work in Acts 5:1-11. The families of many early Christians disowned them, cutting off all their support. As we have stressed throughout this book, people in the ancient world could survive only in the context of their extended family. The only way new Christians could avoid starvation was through the aid of their new family, the church. Church members pooled their resources to help the needy (Acts 4:34-37). God loaned property and resources to believers so they could help those in need.[18] Many sold land or houses and gave the proceeds to the apostles, who distributed it.

Ananias and Sapphira voluntarily sold a piece of property to contribute money to the church poor fund, then decided to keep part of it for themselves (Acts 5:1, 2). When the husband brought the partial gift, Peter asked him why he had let Satan convince him to withhold part of the money (verse 3). The verb "kept back" (verse 2) alludes to the story of Achan (Joshua 7:1), showing the seriousness of Ananias' deed in the mind of the early church. The church member had the right to do whatever he wanted with his property or money, but he was not to lie about it—especially to God (verse 4). After hearing Peter's words Ananias died, and the shocking event frightened all who heard of the incident (verse 5).

When the wife arrived about three hours later, Peter inquired if she and her husband had sold their land for the partial sum Ananias had brought (verses 7, 8). He gave her a chance to confess what the couple had done, but she persisted in the deception. She lied that it had indeed been the actual sale price (verse 8). The apostle then told her that both of them had tried to deceive the Holy Spirit by lying to the church, and now she would die as had her husband (verse 9). When she immediately dropped dead (verse 10), "great fear[19] seized the whole church[20] and all who heard these things" (verse 11).

If the couple had gotten away with their plan, others would have learned about it and tried it themselves. The Christian community had to pool its resources to feed the suddenly homeless believers. They had to learn to honor and care for each other. The struggling infant church could not afford a polarization into haves and have-nots. To prevent the demoralization of the community of faith God had to take highly symbolic and even harsh action. He could not permit church members to think that they could deceive not only each other but God Himself. As with all the stories of people in the Bible, the account of Ananias and

Sapphira serves to illustrate another of the fundmental principles of life and reality.

---

[1] D. Kidner, *Genesis*, p. 135.

[2] This incident is discussed more fully in chapter 9.

[3] *Harper's Bible Commentary*, p. 166.

[4] Some of the following points derive from the observations of Roland Kenneth Harrison in his *Leviticus: An Introduction and Commentary* (Downers Grove, Ill.: InterVarsity Press, 1980), pp. 109, 110.

[5] *Ibid.,* p. 109.

[6] J. Walton and V. Matthews, *IVP Bible Background Commentary: Genesis-Deuteronomy*, p. 154.

[7] Harrison, p. 111.

[8] *Ibid.,* p. 110.

[9] *Harper's Bible Commentary*, p. 258.

[10] W. Brueggemann, *First and Second Samuel*, p. 248.

[11] Baldwin, *1 & 2 Samuel*, p. 208.

[12] R Nelson, *First and Second Kings*, p. 179.

[13] *Ibid.,* p. 182.

[14] D. Wiseman, *1 & 2 Kings*, p. 208.

[15] Nelson, p. 183.

[16] Wiseman, p. 208.

[17] A unit of weight of silver (75-88 pounds or 34-40 kilograms in weight) equal to many years of income.

[18] Christine D. Pohl, *Making Room*, pp. 114, 115.

[19] The modern English translation "great fear" "has become too conventional in our ears to convey the sense of dread that there must have been" (I. Marshall, *The Acts of the Apostles*, p. 112. It was a fear that penetrated to the core and totally shocked the church members.

[20] Luke here for the first time uses the word "church" *(ekklesia)* to describe the Christian community (Marshall, pp. 113, 114). The couple's sin was not just before and against God, but also the people of God.